Living Well, Aging Well

Discover the Profound Beauty and Meaning of Aging

Rev. Jose Kallukalam

LIVING WELL, AGING WELL

A Practical Guide
to
Aging with Wisdom and Vitality

Rev. Jose Kallukalam

FOREWORD BY

MOST REVEREND THOMAS WENSKI
Archbishop of Miami

'Living Well, Aging Well'
Is dedicated to my parents

Thomas J. Kallukalam
&
Mary Thomas Kallukalam

For being the model of Aging Gracefully
And showing that life matters.

Acknowledgements

ACKNOWLEDFEMENTS

I extend my heartfelt gratitude to:
Most Reverend Thomas Wenski,
Archbishop of Miami
for the gracious and inspiring Foreword he so generously contributed
to this book.
Bishop Emeritus Felipe J. Estévez
for his encouragement, inspiration, and constant support in bringing
this work to life.
Guy & Debbie Barg
For their diligent editing of the book.

The Parishioners of St. Michael's
who have shown me, by their lives and witness, how to age gracefully
and whose stories have found their way into these pages.
The Sisters of the Adoration of the Blessed Sacrament
for their spiritual support and practical assistance in the completion
of this book.

My dearest friends
who have always encouraged me to live my retirement years with
purpose and passion.
And above all,
to the Almighty and Loving God
Who chose me—unworthy though I am—as an instrument in His
hands,
entrusting me with the grace and gifts of the Holy Spirit
to serve His people and do something meaningful
with my life.

FOREWORD

The Polish poet, Stanislaw Jerzy Lec (1909-1966) wrote: **"Youth is the gift of nature, but age is a work of art".** Father Jose Kallukalam, a Catholic priest born Kerala, India, is also a bit of a poet having composed lyrics for hundreds of songs. With a rich background in communications gleaned from his studies at Loyola University of Chicago, in this book, Living Well, Aging Well, he offers us, through insightful anecdotes, an understanding of the inevitably of aging (unless we die young) and the pains and joys accompanying the passage of the years.

The reader will find in this short book wisdom, humor, and spiritual uplift. From the perspective of faith, we know that God did not make us just for us to die one day. He made us live with him for all eternity. That hope to live with God for all eternity is what should motivate us throughout our lives to "live well" and "age well" and thus to produce that "work of art" that is a life well lived.

Father Jose has given years of devoted service to his parishioners in northeastern Florida. This book has allowed him to distill some of the experience acquired over those years of service into this book. Sharing these experiences with the reader is a work of art itself. Enjoy!

✠ **Most Reverend Thomas Wenski**
  Archbishop of Miami

Preface

After fifty years of pastoral ministry, a quarter of which as Pastor at St. Michael's Catholic Church, Fernandina Beach, Florida, I entered retired life. This transition sparked a profound contemplation of aging and mortality, a reality that was once a distant horizon. The majority of the people of the parish I retired from, sixty percent, comprises seniors in their retirement, which further deepened my connection to this topic.

In these moments of reflection, I found myself drawn to the questions and contemplations that had long lingered in the background of my pastoral work but now came to the forefront of my personal journey.

What does it mean to age gracefully in the light of faith? How can we find purpose and meaning in our later years? What wisdom does our theology offer us as we face the inevitability of our own mortality? These questions, once theoretical, now feel deeply personal and urgent, not just for me but for all of us who are on this shared journey of aging.

Conversations and pastoral interactions with parishioners over the years had often touched upon the struggles and joys of growing older. I listened to stories of difficult marriages, the pain of losing loved ones, the challenge of maintaining health, and the search for meaning beyond professional accomplishments. These stories were filled with profound spirituality and resilience, yet they also revealed a hunger for a deeper understanding of aging from a theological perspective.

The turning point came during a quiet afternoon a few months into my retirement. I was sitting in my favorite armchair, gazing out at the serene beauty of Fernandina Beach. The tranquility of the scene contrasted sharply with the tumultuous thoughts within me. I realized that my retirement journey was not just about stepping away from active ministry but also into a new role that required me to explore and articulate the spiritual dimensions of aging, a task I felt deeply committed to.

It became clear that this exploration was not only for my benefit but also for the countless individuals who, like me, were navigating the complexities of aging. I felt a calling to delve into the rich tapestry of theological insights on aging, to uncover the spiritual treasures that can guide us through this inevitable phase of life.

This book is the result of that calling, an attempt to weave together personal reflections, scriptural teachings, and theological wisdom to offer a comprehensive understanding of the theology of aging. It is interspersed with gems of real-life stories gathered from my pastoral experience of ministering to my people. Though all of them are stories from the real lives of people I had met over the years, I changed some names to protect their privacy.

In writing this book, I hope to provide solace and inspiration to those embarking on this journey. Whether you are approaching retirement, already living it, or supporting someone who is, I pray that these pages will offer you peace, purpose, and hope. **Aging is not merely a passage of time but a sacred pilgrimage—** a journey that, with faith and understanding, can lead us closer to the heart of God.

Introduction
The Seasons Of The Soul

As I sit down to pen these words, I am humbled by the privilege of embarking on a journey with you that explores the sacred landscape of aging, where the seasons of life unfold with grace, wisdom, and profound meaning.

As a pastor, I have walked alongside individuals and families as they navigated the ebbs and flows of life's journey. From the tender innocence of childhood to the seasoned wisdom of old age, each stage holds its own beauty, challenges, and invitation to encounter the divine. We are all part of this shared human experience, and this connection is what makes our journey through life so profound.

Yet, in the later seasons of life—when the shadows lengthen and the horizon appears with silver linings—we often find ourselves pausing to ponder the mysteries of existence with renewed depth and clarity. In these moments of reflection, the theology of aging comes to life, illuminating the path with insights drawn from life experiences, the shared experiences of humanity, and being enlightened by Scripture.

This book, **"Living Well, Aging Well: Embracing the Theology of Aging,"** is born out of a deep desire to transform the narrative around aging - from something seen as decline, burden, or irrelevance, to something rich with meaning, purpose, wisdom, and spiritual depth. In the pages that follow, we will embark on a voyage of discovery—a journey that invites us to explore the rich tapestry of life as we wrestle with the profound questions of mortality and its meaning.

Each chapter is not just a collection of thoughts but a practical guide designed to offer insights and encouragement to embrace the gifts and challenges of growing older with open hearts and minds. Above all, the biblical perspectives of the entire experience will open our minds to the broader reality of human existence.

But this is more than a theoretical exploration; it is a deeply personal journey—a pilgrimage of the soul. As we delve into the theology of aging, we will inevitably encounter our own fears, hopes, joys, and sorrows reflected in the mirror of lives around us. In this sacred space of vulnerability, we will discover the transformative power of grace, compassion, and community to sustain us on our pilgrimage.

So, dear reader, I invite you to embark on this journey with an open heart and a willing spirit. **Let us walk together, hand in hand, as we navigate the terrain of aging with faith, courage, and a deep reverence for the mystery that lies at the heart of all existence.**

May these words be a beacon of light amidst the shadows, guiding us ever closer to the Source of all life and love.

Chapter 1
Why Think Of Aging?

Aging is an inevitable part of life, yet it is often misunderstood, overlooked, or even feared. Growing older can seem daunting, even unwelcome, in a society that celebrates youth and vigor. But what if we were to shift our perspective and view aging not as a decline but as a sacred journey? **It is a journey filled with potential for growth, wisdom, and a deeper connection with God.**

Embracing aging as a time of profound spiritual growth can inspire and motivate us. What could we discover about ourselves and our faith in this journey? This new perspective could transform our aging experience, making it a time of profound spiritual growth and self-discovery.

As a retired Catholic pastor with decades of pastoral experience, I have walked alongside many individuals through the various stages of life. I have witnessed the joys, sorrows, challenges, and triumphs accompanying aging. I understand the fear and uncertainty that often accompany the thought of aging and mortality.

However, through these experiences, I have seen aging as a profound spiritual journey that invites us into deeper intimacy with

God and a richer understanding of our purpose. Therefore, although many people may not want to discuss aging and mortality, it doesn't go away, like ignoring "the elephant in the room."

If aging and death are inevitable realities, is it better to avoid thinking about them or confront them and handle them with purposeful awareness? Be prepared with adequate knowledge and meaningful tools to handle the reality of aging and death.

Therefore, as a favor to ourselves, we should actively explore the interconnected **physical, mental, and spiritual dimensions of aging.** Recognizing that each aspect is essential to our overall well-being, we should delve into the wisdom that comes with age, the importance of community and relationships, and the hope that our faith provides in the face of mortality. This could involve seeking guidance from spiritual leaders, engaging in community activities, and deepening our understanding of our faith. This holistic approach will enrich our understanding of aging and inspire us to embrace this stage of life with faith and hope.

As Christianity offers the best answers to end-of-life questions and what comes after death, we should discover how aging can be turned into a time of grace, resilience, and profound spiritual growth. Through the lens of Christian theology, which is deeply rooted in Sacred Scripture, we should examine and confront the reality of getting old and saying goodbye to this world. The role of faith in providing hope and grace in the face of mortality can be a source of reassurance and comfort. Isn't it better to be prepared than to be caught off guard?

Chapter 2
Aging - A Physical Phenomenon?

You always thought you were a perfectly fit person physically. You fondly recall **your younger days** when the fields of play were your kingdom, and every victory felt like the conquest of the world. You proudly wore the captain's badge from football fields to basketball courts. The echoes of cheers and the taste of victory still resonate in the corridors of your mind.

However, the landscape drastically changes when the curtain rises in the next act. **As you went to college,** new values and aspirations set in. Sports took a backseat to academics; pursuing knowledge became your new game field. A fire of ambition burned within you, propelling your life to new heights.

Adult Life Dreams

Then came the **rush and bustle of adult life**, bringing a whirlwind of obligations and responsibilities. You started your own business, or readily accepted lucrative jobs, or got involved in the family business. As a result, careers blossomed, families flourished, and days seemed short. You maintained healthy food habits and engaged in some weekend physical activities. You accepted more invitations from your friends or colleagues for parties and hosted some such events, basking in the simple joys of togetherness. Your career and family have been a source of immense pride and fulfillment.

Once **you got married and had children,** the scene dramatically changed. You became a coach for your children's favorite games or went to picnics or beaches with them. You even found time to go hiking with your family and friends. You did not even notice time flying faster. Once, you were eager to grow up as a child and probably thought school days were an eternity. Now, you have no time to do everything you want to do. Your days and hours are divided between work, family, social events, and Church.

Empty Nest

Seasons changed almost imperceptibly, and your life's landscape also changed with it. Suddenly, you realize that your children have grown up, started spreading their wings, and ventured into new skies. They went from school to college, and the reality now strikes you that **you are left with an empty nest that once teemed with youthful energy and laughter.** Your children graduate, seek a job, get engaged, and want to marry and start their own family life. The 'Empty Nest' phase brings a bittersweet mix of nostalgia and longing for the days when your home was filled with the laughter of your children.

After helping them through all these phases of life and feeling grateful for everything you have achieved, you and your spouse see retirement looming on the horizon. Children have moved away and have little time to visit you as often as they want. You and your spouse finally realize caring for the big house has become too much on your plate. Winters feel colder, and bodies become wearier. Yet, there is a sense of relief and anticipation as you prepare for the next phase of your life — retirement.

"We are Moving"

In a quiet acceptance of the inevitable march of time, your spouse wonders aloud, "I think we are getting old." That thought strikes you for a moment like a thunderbolt. "Yes, I, too, feel it. We need to take it easy now. Let us sell this big house and move somewhere we don't have to deal with this snow and freezing weather." Your spouse responds, "True. I cannot get my body to go everywhere I want anymore. And I have developed some back pain lately." That sealed the decision. "We are moving," both of you said in unison. Though not easy, this decision was necessary to prepare for the next phase of your life.

You find a perfect place where the temperature is not too cold, taxes are low, and living conditions are better. You settle in an affordable house in a nice neighborhood, make new friends, and find a warm and welcoming Church. Your physical activity now shifts to golfing, and a different lifestyle starts. Though you want to get involved in various Church or community activities, you notice a change in your energy levels and enthusiasm. This shift, while expected, is a reminder of the physical and mental changes that come with retirement.

Chapter 3
Once, On A Quiet Evening

On a tranquil evening, you and your spouse bask in the soft glow of twilight, a glass of wine in your hands, and the air is filled with a serene sense of contentment. The day's bustle has given way to a peaceful stillness, a perfect backdrop for reflection. As you sip your wine, your thoughts drift to the long, winding journey that has brought the two of you to this very moment.

The Weight of Words

You muse aloud with a touch of wisdom gleaned from years of shared experiences, "I think it was wise that we wrote our will. Who knows what might happen to us!" Your voice is gentle, yet the words carry the weight of deep contemplation.

Your spouse, ever attuned to the subtleties in your tone, looks up and meets your gaze. "I have noticed that you mention it more frequently in your conversations. Are you worried about something? Do you know something that I don't know?" The concern in her eyes is unmistakable, a reflection of the bond you both cherish.

"Not really," you reply, your voice steady but introspective. "Only because it is the reality we must face sooner or later." Your words evoke a quiet acceptance, a recognition of the inevitable passage of time, bringing a sense of reassurance and calm.

Rising from the chair with a gentle sigh, your spouse says, "We will discuss it more tomorrow. I feel tired. Let us go to bed." The evening's tranquility wraps around you both like a comforting blanket as you make your way to the bedroom, bringing a sense of relaxation and ease.

The Truth

However, long after the lights are turned off, your words still echo in your ears. As you lay staring into the darkened ceiling, your mind wanders deeper into the truths you had spoken. "Isn't it the truth?" you think. "In many ways, my body and mind tell me that."

In the stillness of the night, you come to a profound realization. Aging is not just about the physical transformations—the graying hair, the deepening lines, the slowing pace—but also about the profound shifts in your mental and spiritual dimensions. Aging, you understand, is a multifaceted phenomenon. It is not merely a physical journey but a journey of the soul.

You find solace in this awareness, understanding that each wrinkle and scar tell a tale—a testament to a life well-lived, filled with moments of joy, sorrow, love, and loss. Each line etched on your face is a chapter in your story, each scar a reminder of battles fought and won.

A Journey

Aging is a journey of reflection, resilience, and grace. It offers endless opportunities for growth and transformation. You feel a profound sense of peace as you lay there, listening to the gentle rhythm of your spouse's breathing. You realize that the interconnected dimensions of aging—physical, mental, and spiritual—each play a crucial role in shaping the human experience.

And so, in the quiet darkness, you find yourself embracing the journey with all its challenges and rewards. You understand that **aging is not something to be feared but a testament to a**

life rich with experiences, a heart full of reminiscences, and a spirit ready for the transformations yet to come.......

Therefore, dear reader, it is essential to understand the physical, cognitive, and spiritual dimensions of aging and be prepared to handle them when the time comes. The following chapters provide an in-depth understanding of this subject and practical tips and guidance.

<u>Tailpiece</u>

An elderly woman was sitting on the patio one evening, enjoying a glass of wine with her husband. She said, "I love you so much. I don't know how I could ever live without you."

Her husband asked, "Is that you or the wine talking?"

She replied, "Of course, it's me talking to the wine."

Chapter 4
Understanding Physical Aging

U nderstanding the physical dimensions of aging is not just informative but also empowering. It helps us prepare for the inevitable changes that occur as our bodies age, such as the gradual decline of physical strength and stamina and the emergence of age-related health issues.

The Changes

One of the more common changes that occur with aging is the natural decline of muscle strength, known as 'sarcopenia.' This often leads to decreased mobility and balance issues, and we see older people frequently falling. Another common issue is the decline in bone health, coinciding with a reduction of bone density, known as 'osteoporosis.'

As a result, people who have advanced in age become more vulnerable to bone fractures. Joint aches due to the wear down of cartilage are also an everyday companion of old age. Lastly, the cardiovascular system is often affected by age, with some of its effects being the stiffening of blood vessels, decreased elasticity of heart muscle, and increased risk of hypertension and heart disease.

As we age, our metabolic rate tends to slow down, often leading to weight gain and accelerating knee and hip pain and back aches. However, these issues can be managed with the right lifestyle choices. Aging also brings about vision and hearing problems, such as difficulty focusing on close objects and understanding speech, which can be frustrating. However, these issues can be mitigated with the help of corrective measures.

Among the most visible signs of aging, the most notable are skin changes. As skin loses its elasticity and thins, it leads to wrinkles and an increased risk of injury. However, a good skincare routine can help maintain skin health. Additionally, reduced immune function in old age can increase susceptibility to infections and slower wound healing, but a healthy lifestyle and regular medical check-ups can help manage these risks.

Challenges:

Health Declines: As we age, we may face chronic conditions such as arthritis, which causes joint pain and stiffness; cardiovascular diseases, which affect the heart and blood vessels; and osteoporosis. These conditions are prevalent in aging individuals, involving a significant portion of the population. Mobility issues and sensory impairments like vision and hearing loss are also common.

Energy Levels: Reduced stamina and energy can limit our daily activities and impact the overall quality of life.

Physical Appearance: The changes in physical appearance, such as wrinkles and graying hair, can affect self-esteem and body image.

Opportunities:

Alongside the challenges of aging come meaningful opportunities to counterbalance its effects—through healthy lifestyle choices, proactive health management, and the use of adaptive aids that support independence and well-being.

Healthy Living: Despite its challenges, aging allows us to focus on a healthier lifestyle. It is common knowledge that regular exercise, balanced nutrition, and adequate sleep are essential and can enhance physical well-being. Our bodies showcase remarkable resilience as they age, reminding us of our strength and potential.

This resilience can inspire hope and motivate us to take care of our health.

Proactive Health Management: Regular medical check-ups and screenings are not just about detecting health issues early; they're about taking control of our health and improving our longevity and quality of life. By being proactive, we can stay one step ahead of potential health problems, empowering us to make informed decisions about our well-being. This sense of control can empower us to take charge of our health and well-being.

Adaptation and Aids: Technological advancements such as smart home devices and wearable health trackers can help maintain independence and mobility. Adaptive devices like walking canes, hearing aids, and magnifying glasses can also significantly improve daily life for aging individuals. These aids can provide support and reassurance, making daily life more manageable and enjoyable.

Practical Advice:

Stay Active: Engage in regular physical activities suited to your ability level, such as walking, swimming, or yoga. This is crucial for maintaining strength, flexibility, and cardiovascular health as you age.

Balanced Diet: Dieticians ask us to follow a healthy diet that includes fresh fruits, vegetables, whole grains, lean proteins, and healthy fats such as those in fish. Avoid processed foods and sugar.

Health Management: Following medical advice, taking prescribed medications, and attending regular health screenings are essential. These screenings are not just routine; they are your proactive steps toward a healthy future. Stay informed about your health conditions and treatments. This practical advice is not just a list of tasks but a roadmap to your health and well-being, designed to give you the confidence and security you need to navigate the challenges of aging.

Aging can cause a shift in emotional well-being, potentially leading to depression and anxiety. Recognizing and addressing these emotional changes is crucial in managing physical health. In the next chapter, you will read the story of a couple who effectively addressed their serious illness and faced the inevitable reality.

<u>Tailpiece</u>

At a bustling weekend restaurant, an elderly couple arrived with a mix of determination and a touch of humor. After a spirited struggle from the car, the husband cheerfully announced, "We're Joe and Mary."

The hostess apologized, "I'm afraid there's a 15-minute wait for a table."

With a knowing smile, the husband quipped, "Young lady, at our age, I don't think we have that much time left!"

In no time at all, they were shown to their table.

Chapter 5
Looking Beyond
Physical Problems

The **Sliders,** a couple in their late sixties, were active members of the parish, enjoying travel, family, and friends. Both were in their second marriages and embraced life with gratitude and enthusiasm. Everything seemed wonderful—until George was diagnosed with advanced cancer.

When they shared the devastating news with me, both were in tears and I, too, was deeply saddened, as we had become good friends. Yet, as their pastor, I knew my role was not just to grieve with them but to guide them spiritually.

Embracing the Reality, Not the Fear

I encouraged them to view their situation through the lens of faith, presenting them with two choices:

1. **Succumb to sadness and fear**, allowing the diagnosis to overshadow their remaining time.
2. **Accept the reality,** seek the best medical care, and live fully, cherishing every moment together.

They chose the second. Instead of withdrawing into despair, they embraced life even more fully, strengthening their faith and leaning on God's promises.

I urged them to incorporate Bible reading and prayer into their daily routine, reminding them of Jesus' comforting words about God's providential care:

"Are not five sparrows sold for two small coins? And yet, God has not forgotten one of these. Even the very hairs of your head have all been numbered. Therefore, do not be afraid. You are worth more than many sparrows." (Luke 12:6-7)

I also encouraged them to reflect on **Matthew 6:25-34**, where Jesus tells us:

"Do not be anxious about tomorrow, for the future day will be anxious for itself." (Matthew 6:34)

These passages helped reframe their perspective, leading them to surrender their worries to God and focus on the gift of the present moment.

Living Fully Despite the Diagnosis

Months passed, and nearly a year later, Joan called with a request —George wanted to see me and receive the Sacrament of the Anointing of the Sick.

When I visited, George was physically weak but spiritually strong. With peace reflected in his voice, he said, "Father, I think my time has come. That's what the doctor says, and I feel it." Yet, there was no fear, only acceptance.

Joan shared how they had made the most of the past year, continuing to travel and enjoy life despite the illness. Their story was a testament to hope, faith, and gratitude—proof that joy is possible even in the shadow of death.

I anointed George and gave him the Eucharist, the true food for the journey. Three days later, he peacefully passed away.

. . .

A Legacy of Faith and Gratitude

At George's funeral, Joan expressed deep gratitude for the new perspective they had embraced. Instead of fearing the inevitable, they had chosen to live fully, cherishing every moment as a gift from God.

Their journey was a powerful reminder that while we cannot control the length of our lives, we can choose how we live them. We can face even the most significant challenges of life with grace and peace if we have faith and trust in God's plan.

(This story has a sequel coming later.)

Chapter 6
Body And Mind

It is a profound truth that every human being is not just a physical entity but a divine amalgamation of body and soul. This understanding, often referred to as the mind, Spirit, or soul in religious contexts, goes beyond its philosophical or psychological implications. Genesis 1:26-27 affirms that God uniquely fashioned humans as a harmonious blend of physical and spiritual elements.

Numerous Scripture passages, including Ecclesiastes 12:7, Matthew 10:28, 1 Corinthians 4:16, 7:1, and James 2:22, bear witness to this truth. Genesis 2:7 vividly depicts this creation, stating, "And then the Lord God formed man from the clay of the earth, and He breathed into his face the breath of life, and man became a living soul."

The age-old philosophical debate about whether humanity is dichotomous (body and Spirit) or trichotomous (body, soul, and Spirit) is a question that transcends the scope of this discourse. However, the Catechism of the Catholic Church, a comprehensive and authoritative source, offers a perspective that is sufficient for our purpose.

It proclaims, **"The human body shares in the dignity of the image of God. It is a human body precisely because a spiritual soul animates it, and it is the whole person intended to become, in the body of Christ, a temple of the Spirit."** (CCC 364) The Catechism further elucidates that 'Spirit' signifies that from creation, man is ordered to a supernatural end and that his soul can gratuitously be raised, beyond all it deserves, to communion with God.

Mind-Body Dichotomy

The interaction between a person's mind and body is a mysterious phenomenon that significantly influences their health. The mind-body problem, as articulated by the French philosopher **Rene Descartes**, continues to intrigue philosophers to this day. Jonathan Westphal[1] aptly notes that the properties of mind and body are very different, like oil and water, which won't mix. Descartes stated that matter is fundamentally spatial. Objects in space have a position and height, length, and width. Mental entities, the spirit, lack these spatial attributes.

This mind-body problem was discussed long before Descartes. Philosophers and religious thinkers have spoken about the body and mind or soul and their relationship. Ancient Greek philosopher **Plato,** for example, wrote in his dialogue (Phaedo) about the soul's survival after death and its immortality. Rather than saying how the soul exists in the body or leaves it, his emphasis was on the fact that the soul survives death.

This concept got better clarity later when Christian theologians explained it in the light of the Sacred Scriptures. For example, **St. Thomas Aquinas a**grees with Plato and says that the soul is immortal, immaterial, and a spiritual form. Aquinas saw life as a gift from God to be loved, nurtured, and lived in proper charity.

What God has Revealed

---

1. Jonathan Westpool - The Mind-Body Problem - MIT Press Essential Knowledge series

What we know about the relationship between body and soul and what happens to them when we die are only as much as what God has revealed to us. We see a complete and convincing revelation of this reality in what Jesus said and did.

In Summary

God, in His divine image, creates human beings with both body and soul. The soul transcends mortality at death while the body returns to dust. Through Jesus' death and resurrection, God promises to raise us to eternity. St. Paul proclaims, "Now Christ has risen again from the dead, as the first-fruits of those who sleep." (1 Cor. 15:10) And again, "For the trumpet will sound, and the dead will rise up, incorruptible. And we shall be transformed." (1 Cor. 15:52) Eternity is a gracious gift from God. Yet, its quality is influenced by the life we lead on earth. **(Matthew 25: 31-46)**

The real story in the next chapter illustrates how someone who deeply believed that eternal life is more important than earthly existence lived out that faith. He understood that we leave all material possessions behind and that the true significance lies in the eternity of our souls.

Chapter 7
A Man Of Few Needs

Father **Gerald O'Shea,** a retired Lieutenant Commander of the Navy Chaplains' Corps, arrived at St. Michael's Church in Fernandina Beach to fill in when the pastor was transferred. Even after the new pastor settled in, Father Gerry stayed, always willing to assist. When I later became pastor, he graciously continued serving, never seeking recognition, just quietly giving of himself.

Every Saturday afternoon, he'd arrive at the rectory, assist with the Saturday evening Mass, stay overnight, and handle one of the Sunday Masses. Over time, a simple tradition formed—our Saturday night dinners at a local restaurant.

A Simple Soul with a Simple Routine

"Father Gerry, where do you want to go for dinner?" I'd ask.

His response never changed: **"Wherever you want."**

I'd shake my head, smiling. "That's no help, Father."

He was content with whatever was placed before him, never one to demand or complain. He knew his role at the parish was essential, but he never acted as though he were indispensable.

"Father, would you like to start with a glass of wine?" I'd ask.

His reply was always the same: "Sure."

A Man Who Needed Nothing

The parishioners adored their priests and were incredibly generous, especially around Christmas and birthdays. Father Gerry, however, always insisted:

"Please ask people not to give me anything. I have plenty of money."

His Navy pension covered his needs, and he saw no reason to accumulate more. Yet, this same man who had "plenty of money" would rush to McDonald's every Sunday morning—just for the senior discount coffee.

He lived modestly, in a small, low-cost apartment near Jacksonville's Mayport area, just as he had in his naval chaplaincy days. He never sought luxury, finding contentment in simplicity.

The Chaplain's Mass and the Sunday Comics

Father Gerry's approach to Mass was straightforward. His years in the Navy had shaped him—he wasn't overly meticulous about rituals or the precise use of sacred vessels.

"We had only 30 minutes to prepare for Mass and do everything else," he explained once. *"Sometimes, we didn't even have a proper altar."*

His homilies were brief—to the point, practical, and often laced with humor. He loved comic strips, especially Snoopy, Sgt. Snorkel, and Hagar the Horrible.

Every Sunday over breakfast, he'd cut out comic strips from the *newspaper. Without fail, he'd ask:*

"Can I cut this one out?"

And, just as predictably, I'd mimic his response: "Sure."

He kept thousands of these comics, neatly stored in trash bags in his closet, as if they were precious relics of joy.

A Jubilee Celebration and a Declining Body

The parish celebrated his Golden Jubilee with great joy. Father Gerry had hoped to travel to the New York Archdiocese to celebrate his 50th anniversary with his seminary classmates, but by then, he was too weak from multiple bypass surgeries.

We urged him to stay closer to the church, where we could check on him more frequently, but he refused to be a burden.

"I'll be fine," he always said.

A Quiet Departure

One morning, the cleaning lady found him lying on the floor of his apartment, unable to get up. He had been there for over twelve hours.

After a few days in the hospital, he was moved to a nursing home, where he spent his final days. When his family cleaned out his apartment, they found nothing of material value—

- A few pieces of low-cost furniture,
- Minimal appliances,
- A small TV,
- A landline phone,
- Clothes not even worth donating.

Even in his room at the rectory, his possessions were few—just some clothes and bags of Sunday comics.

A Life of Humility and Grace

Father Gerry lived as he preached—a man of few needs who saw no value in wealth or possessions.

His life embodied Jesus' words:

"Blessed are the poor in spirit, for theirs is the kingdom of God." (Matthew 5:3)

He left behind no grand legacy, only a quiet but powerful testimony of humility, dedication, and a heart filled with contentment. And people loved him.

In the world's eyes, he died in simplicity, not grandeur.

But in God's eyes, he left behind everything for what truly mattered.

Chapter 8
Exploring Mental Health
In Aging

As every human being is a composite of body and mind, paying attention to the mental dimensions of aging is essential and key to a fulfilling and vibrant life. The importance of maintaining mental and emotional well-being alongside physical health cannot be overstated. It is paramount for overall quality of life and vitality and should be a top priority as we age.

Cognitive Health and emotional well-being encompass various mental processes such as memory, reasoning, attention, and decision-making. These naturally change as people age. In contrast, emotional well-being is related to our emotional resilience, ability to manage stress, and overall mood stability.

Despite the challenging myths and misconceptions surrounding mental health issues related to cognitive aging, psychology and neuroscience offer empowering insights. This knowledge not only equips us with strategies to maintain mental sharpness, resilience, and emotional balance in later life but also instills a sense of control over the aging process.

Some of these strategies include regular physical exercise, engaging in mentally stimulating activities, maintaining a healthy diet, and seeking social support.[1] Recognizing that a complex interaction of biological and psychological factors contributes to emotional distress and cognitive decline is essential. By relying on the latest findings and developments in mental health research, we can access resources that are now available to assist us with our mental well-being.

Understand Cognitive Aging

Psychology studies human behavior—how we think, feel, and behave. Neuroscience is the study of the brain and nervous system. Both provide insights into how our minds and brains work and change as we age.

When we refer to cognitive aging, it means the changes that happen to our mental faculties, such as memory, attention, and problem-solving, as people age. Neuroscience tells us that some brain regions shrink and become less efficient, resulting in the decline of our cognitive functions. Other factors such as genetics, lifestyle habits (for example, diet and exercise), stressful life, or social isolation also accelerate cognitive aging.

It is proven that staying physically active and engaging in mentally stimulating activities, such as doing puzzles or learning a new skill, helps preserve older peoples' cognitive function.[2]

In the next chapter, you will meet a couple who faced a serious cognitive aging problem, Alzheimer's. This chapter is not just about a battle against an unrelenting disease. It is about the enduring power of love, the strength in vulnerability, and the beauty of cherishing every fleeting moment together. Despite being the greatest challenge of their life, the enveloping love of the husband and wife sets an excellent example for everyone, inspiring hope, and resilience in the face of cognitive aging challenges.

---

1. Neighbors who care network- 'Unlocking the Mind'
2. Senex Memory Advisors - Syed Rizvi 'Understanding Cognitive Decline'

Chapter 9
A Love Remembered

Tim and Janet had been married for over fifty years. Their story was the kind that young lovers dream of, filled with shared laughter and countless memories.

One morning, Tim noticed that Janet had forgotten to make their morning coffee, a ritual she had done without fail for decades. She loved her morning coffee, and so did Tim. Over time, these minor lapses became more frequent, and Janet was diagnosed with Alzheimer's disease. The news was devastating, and Tim faced the daunting task of caring for his beloved wife as her memory slipped away. Yet, his resolve to care for her with the same unwavering love he had always shown was admirable.

They maintained their weekly routine of going to church together, a tradition deeply rooted in their faith and their love for each other. Tim ensured that Janet took the check in the offertory envelope, a small act symbolizing their shared responsibilities and enduring bond. She would smile and say, "You know I wouldn't forget that." On the way back, they would discuss what the priest had said in the homily and wondered whether their children went to church. Sometimes, Tim would get a call from the parish office regarding some of the mistakes on the check, but he would discreetly handle it, never letting Janet know.

As the years passed, Janet's condition worsened. She began to forget their children's names and the stories she once loved to tell. But Tim, unwavering and incredibly patient, remained by her side. Each day, he would brew coffee for her and take her to the garden, where they had spent countless mornings together. Their love and memories were still alive in his mind, creating a warm and nostalgic atmosphere.

Every night, Tim would read to Janet from her beloved poetry book, share dinner, and finally, before bed, read a passage from the Bible and say their usual prayers. His voice would weave through the verses, sometimes eliciting a soft smile from Janet. In these moments, Tim found solace, knowing that the essence of their love still lingered, deep and unshakable.

One evening, as sunlight filtered through the window blinds, Tim noticed Janet gazing at him and whispering, "Thank you for loving me." These simple words, filled with gratitude and love, pierced through the fog of Alzheimer's and reminded Tim of their enduring bond. Tears welled up in Tim's eyes, and he held her close, feeling the warmth of her embrace.

Some of his friends asked Tim why he wouldn't move Janet to the memory care unit of the nearby nursing home. It would be easier for him, and she would get professional care there. With a smile, Tim said, "Would the people at the nursing home be able to give her a husband's loving care?" They replied, "She no longer knows you are her husband." He said, "But I know she is my wife."

Tim continued to care for Janet with unwavering devotion until the end of her days. For Tim, love was not bound by the frailty of memory but was a divine thread that connected them beyond the limits of time and space. He always cherished what he had promised her at their wedding: "I promise to be faithful to you in good times and in bad, in sickness and in health. I will love you and honor you all the days of my life."

Living Well, Aging Well

In the twilight of his life, Tim would often sit in their garden, reading from the same Bible, feeling Janet's presence in every verse. Their love story, marked by faith and resilience, became a testament to the enduring power of love and the profound theology of aging. For Tim, taking care of Janet was not just an act of duty; it was a sacred and living prayer that celebrated the sanctity of their vows and the divine grace that had woven their lives together.

Chapter 10
Nurture Emotional Well-Being

Our emotional health is a testament to our ability to cope with stress, control our emotions, and nurture positive feelings. Emotional stability, an essential aspect of emotional well-being, is our ability to maintain a consistent emotional state regardless of external circumstances.[1] Research in psychology and neuroscience reveals a positive aspect of aging —as we age, we often gain emotional stability and resilience. Older adults seem to have better resilience to stress and more emotional stability than younger ones. This could be due to their life experience or the changes in brain function. These findings offer a hopeful perspective on aging, suggesting that emotional well-being can improve with time.

The latest research in psychology and neuroscience provides a roadmap to understanding the factors that affect our mental well-being as we age. With this knowledge, we can form habits promoting brain health and maintaining mental well-being. It's also important to note that meaningful relationships, family and social support, and a

---

1. Fabian - Blog Post - 'Motivation Vs Discipline'

sense of purpose are key factors in maintaining emotional well-being in older adults.

Challenges:

- **Cognitive Decline**: Aging can cause changes in cognitive function, including memory loss, slower information processing, and reduced problem-solving abilities. However, it's important to remember that older adults often demonstrate remarkable resilience in adapting to these changes.
- **Mental Health:** Older adults may face mental health issues such as depression, anxiety, and loneliness, often exacerbated by social isolation and loss of loved ones.

Opportunities:

- **Lifelong Learning:** Aging presents an empowering opportunity to engage in lifelong learning, which keeps the mind active and improves cognitive function, fostering continuous growth and development. This is not just a necessity but a chance to explore new horizons and keep the mind sharp, inspiring a sense of purpose and motivation.
- **Social Engagement:** Maintaining and fostering social connections is not just a pleasant pastime but a powerful way to enhance mental well-being and providing emotional support. Social engagement can encourage older adults to prioritize their social connections, fostering a sense of belonging and support.
- **Mindfulness and Stress Reduction**: Practices like quiet reflection, meditation, and relaxation techniques can promote mental health and emotional resilience.

Practical Advice:

- **Mental Stimulation:** Engage in activities that challenge your brain, such as puzzles, reading, learning new skills, or taking up a new hobby. Continuous learning keeps the mind sharp.
- **Stay Connected:** Maintain relationships with family, friends, and community. Join clubs, volunteer, or participate in group activities to combat loneliness and isolation.
- **Seek Support:** Seeking professional help is not a sign of weakness, rather, a proactive step towards addressing mental health challenges. Personal counseling and support groups can provide valuable assistance and coping strategies. This emphasis on the role of professional help can normalize seeking assistance, reassuring the aging that they are not alone in their journey toward mental well-being.[2]

In Summary

While insights from psychology and neuroscience provide valuable information about cognitive aging and emotional well-being in later life, proactive steps to support people's mental well-being and advocating for an age-friendly society are also crucial.

Tailpiece

After dinner one evening, an elderly couple settled in to watch their favorite show. "Ernie, what would you like from the kitchen?" his wife called out.

"Two scoops of ice cream with extra chocolate syrup, please," he replied. "You'd better write that down; you seem to forget a lot now."

"I never forget a thing," she boasted.

After what felt like an eternity, she returned—with a bowl of

---

2. Fitness Goal 4 U, December 2024

cereal and milk. Shaking his head with affectionate exasperation, the husband said, "Dear, I told you to write it down—you forgot my toast!"

Chapter 11
Aging In A Secular World
The Challenge Of Faith In Modern Culture

I n an era where secularism dominates much of public discourse, aging has become a concept intertwined with loss—loss of productivity, loss of relevance, and, ultimately, the loss of life itself. Modern culture, heavily focused on youth, beauty, and efficiency, tends to see aging as something to be resisted or ignored rather than embraced. This chapter explores how seniors can navigate these cultural shifts with faith, becoming countercultural witnesses of hope, resilience, and divine purpose.

1. Secular Attitudes Toward Aging: A Cultural Shift

- **The rise of materialism**, consumerism, and individualism has shaped how society views aging.
- **Youth-centric advertising**, cosmetic industries, and anti-aging movements reinforce the idea that growing older is something to delay, hide, or avoid.
- **The devaluation of elders** in modern society contrasts with biblical and historical traditions where wisdom was revered.

. . .

2. The Fear of Aging and Death: A Spiritual Crisis

- Many secular societies see death as the ultimate defeat rather than as a transition into eternal life.
- The loss of faith in an afterlife leads to existential despair, increased anxiety, and a desperate clinging to youth.
- Faith offers a different narrative that sees aging as a sacred journey, not a decline, thereby eliminating the reason to fear.

3. How Faith Counters the Secular Fear of Aging

- **Embracing a Theology of Aging:** Viewing old age as a gift rather than a curse.
- **Wisdom as a Spiritual Asset:** Biblical examples of elders who played critical roles in salvation history (e.g., Simeon and Anna in the Temple, Moses leading at 80, Sarah giving birth in old age).
- **Aging as a Time of Deepening Relationship with God:** Old age is an invitation to prayer, contemplation, and service rather than withdrawal from life.

4. Being a Witness of Hope in a World Focused on Youth and Productivity

- **Living as a Testament to God's Faithfulness:** Demonstrating through one's life the power of faith, trust, and perseverance.
- **Mentoring Younger Generations:** Passing on faith, wisdom, and experiences rather than seeing old age as a time of irrelevance.
- **Resisting the Culture of Fear:** Finding joy and fulfillment in growing older rather than succumbing to societal pressure to maintain youthfulness at all costs.

5. Practical Ways to Live Faithfully in a Secular World

- **Engaging in Intergenerational Dialogue:** Creating bridges between youth and elders to counteract societal division.
- **Using Modern Technology to Evangelize:** Encouraging seniors to use digital platforms to share faith and wisdom.
- **Reclaiming Elders' Role in the Church:** Advocating for ministries that recognize and utilize the spiritual gifts of older adults.

Chapter 12
Societal View Of Mental Aging

Is it possible for an older adult to stay psychologically fit and sharp? Yes, if they adopt practical strategies to help maintain mental sharpness, emotional balance, and resilience. Engaging in regular cognitive exercises that stimulate mental agility and flexibility are some of the steps nursing homes and rehabilitation centers usually adopt.

Being involved in other activities such as meditation, relaxation techniques, building social connections, and making interactions can enhance emotional resilience and well-being. Older adults who live alone should incorporate these into their daily routine to proactively keep up their mental health and thus psychologically flourish in their later lives.

If they can make the trip, Church organizations are excellent venues for seniors to maintain mental agility. They provide them with the opportunity to engage in brain-stimulating activities that not only keep their minds sharp but also bolster social connections and meaningful relationships. These activities can inspire and motivate older adults to improve their mental and emotional well-being, leading to a fulfilling and meaningful life as they age with resilience, optimism, and vitality.

Stigma and Misconceptions

It is crucial to be aware of the stigma and misconceptions surrounding mental health issues of aging people. Stigma in this context refers to negative attitudes, stereotypes, misconceptions, and biases associated with mental health issues. One of the most observed misconceptions is that mental health problems are a normal part of aging. Many people think older people cannot recover from mental health problems. It may prevent older people from seeking assistance and accessing the necessary care and support.

Then, there is another stigma called **ageism**, which means prejudice and discrimination against people based on their age. Stereotyping older adults as being frail, incompetent, or burdensome is also ageism. It will lead to treating them with disparity in accessing healthcare, social support, or opportunities for participation in society.

In practical life, these misconceptions become manifest in various ways:

1. Aged people hesitate to seek help for mental health issues because of the fear of being labeled "senile" or "crazy."
2. Healthcare providers overlook the mental health symptoms of older people, attributing them to the normal aging process rather than addressing them.
3. **Family members or caregivers ignore the emotional issues** of the people in their later life as a normal part of the aging process rather than offering support and solutions.
4. Society and media **portray older adults as forgetful** and, therefore, incompetent and burdensome.

Society, as well as individuals, have a responsibility to address these misconceptions. By promoting education and creating awareness about the mental health issues of old age, we can foster an environment of acceptance and support. This is not just about knowledge but about compassion and empathy. It's about making intentional efforts to promote policies and practices that prioritize practical measures to deal with the mental well-being of older adults. Doing so can create a society where older adults feel valued, supported, and empowered to seek the assistance they need to thrive.

Tailpiece

At their weekly bridge game, an elderly couple bantered, "I've discovered the secret to a long life—laughter and a few extra naps!

The husband added, "No wonder our games last three hours—I'm laughing, and you're napping!"

They both agreed that sometimes the best move is to relax and enjoy the moment.

Chapter 13
Spiritual Dimension Of Aging

The journey of growing old is often overlooked as a source of profound opportunities for spiritual growth. However, exploring the unique spiritual challenges and blessings of aging is crucial. This exploration can help rediscover the meaning and purpose of life, cultivate a sense of gratitude and acceptance of reality, and deepen the relationship with God.

There are numerous **ways to foster spiritual well-being,** such as engaging in prayer and meditation, seeking spiritual guidance and counseling, and participating in the religious services of our faith. These practices can lead us to discover pathways to wholeness and fulfillment in our later life stages, creating a holistic approach to aging that interconnects our body, mind, and spirit. This approach can instill in us a belief that aging is not a journey to be feared or avoided but rather a sacred pilgrimage of growth, wisdom, and love.

Where to Start?

The starting point of the spiritual dimension is a logical discernment about the purpose of life. Will our lives end up in the grave, or is there something beyond it? If someone believes there is nothing to look forward to after death, their life will end up in total despair.

From earlier discussions, we have concluded that there is no answer to the existence of the spiritual component of human life if we do not perceive its continued existence after the death of the material body.

Therefore, the logical conclusion is that we should look forward to the existence of the spirit beyond the death of the body and be prepared to embrace it fully. This is not just a conclusion but an inspiration to live a life transcending the material world.

It means we do whatever our faith offers to secure the eternal life for which the spirit is created. However, it is essential to note that the spirit is the person itself, liberated from the constraints of the body— i.e., time and space. Remember that Jesus' risen body passed through the locked door of the place where the disciples were. Even though we are not God like Jesus, we will also have a resurrected life in Jesus and a spiritual existence with God for all eternity.

St. Paul on Resurrection

Engaging in spiritual reflection, mainly through reading St. Paul's teachings about resurrection in his **letter to the Corinthians**, is a powerful tool for transformation. Take a moment to read and reflect on it carefully, and you will find a source of hope and empowerment.

"Someone may say, "How do the dead rise again?" Or, "What type of body do they return with?" How foolish! What you sow cannot be brought back to life unless it dies.

And what you sow is not the body that will be in the future but a bare grain, such as wheat or some other grain. God gives it a body according to His will and according to each seed's proper body.

Not all flesh is the same flesh. But one is indeed of men, another truly is of beasts, another is of birds, and another is of fish.

Also, there are heavenly bodies and earthly bodies. But while one certainly has the glory of heaven, the other has the glory of earth. One has the brightness of the sun, another the brightness of the moon, and another the brightness of the stars, and one star differs from another star in brightness.

So, it is also with the resurrection of the dead. What is sown in dishonor shall rise to glory. What is sown in weakness shall rise to power. What is sown in an animal body shall rise with a spiritual body. If there is an animal body, there is also a spiritual one. (1 Corinthians 15: 35-45)

".... the dead will rise up, incorruptible. And we shall be transformed." (1 Corinthians 15: 52)

This holistic approach will enable aging adults to embrace the richness and complexity of the human experience, where **physical, mental, and spiritual dimensions converge** in a tapestry of growth, resilience, and transformation. The next chapter will deal with practical steps to adopt in the light of these thoughts.

Chapter 14
From Spiritual Awareness To Action

Contemplating the spiritual dimension of our lives can be transformative, turning aging from an endpoint into a gateway to deeper understanding, greater wisdom, and profound communion with the divine. This realization can infuse the aging process with a sense of fulfillment, courage, and steadfast trust in the unfathomable mystery of life, fostering an optimistic outlook. Now, we consider the spiritual challenges people encounter in their twilight years, how to transform them into opportunities, and how to be practical.

Challenges:

Spiritual Crisis: Aging, with its inherent challenges, can trigger existential questions and a crisis of faith, especially in the face of illness, loss, or nearing the end of life.

Isolation from Faith Communities: Physical limitations or health issues may restrict participation in religious services or activities, leading to spiritual isolation.

Opportunities:

Spiritual Growth: The later years present a unique opportunity for spiritual growth, reflection, and deepening of faith. This period, often associated with challenges, can also be a time of profound spiritual development.

Legacy and Purpose: Aging invites individuals to consider their spiritual legacy, a testament to their faith and beliefs, and find new purposes that align with their values and beliefs. This legacy is a source of pride and significance.

Connection with God: Engage in spiritual practices that can strengthen one's connection with God, offering comfort, peace, and a sense of belonging.

Practical Advice:

Daily Practices: Incorporate spiritual practices in the daily routine, such as prayer, meditation, or reading Sacred Scripture. These practices can provide solace and a sense of routine.

Faith Community: Stay connected with your Church or a spiritual community that is able and willing to understand and support your spiritual journey. Whether through virtual services, phone calls, or small gatherings, seek ways to remain involved. This connection is a vital source of support and care for your spiritual well-being.

Reflect and Serve: Reflect on your life's journey by reviewing your past experiences, lessons learned, and personal growth. Then, consider the various ways in which you can continue contributing to your Church and community. Volunteering, mentoring, or simply sharing your wisdom can provide a sense of purpose and fulfillment.

In practical terms, reflection or mindfulness can be as simple as taking a daily walk in nature, allowing your senses to absorb the vibrant colors and subtle sounds around you, or setting aside a few minutes each morning to sit in quiet reflection. Journaling your thoughts, practicing gratitude, or even engaging in guided meditation can serve as tools to build this inner resilience. Over time, these practices help transform moments of uncertainty into opportunities for growth, turning challenges into stepping stones on your journey toward emotional well-being.

In Summary

The preceding chapters address the physical, mental, and spiritual aspects of aging and provide a comprehensive guide to navigating the aging process with grace and resilience. Each dimension offers unique challenges and opportunities, but we can transform these years into meaningful growth and profound fulfillment with practical advice and a positive outlook.

In the next chapter, we delve into the poignant journey of a family beset by a relentless series of tragedies. Their unwavering faith in God and the steadfast support of their friends became their anchors in the storm. Through their story of faith, courage, and resilience, we witness the profound strength of the human spirit and the grace that accompanies those who trust in something greater than themselves.

Chapter 15
Fighting the Good Fight

When I first arrived at St. Michael's, my first sick call was to **Dr. George,** a physician battling cancer. Despite his illness, he remained optimistic, even jokingly saying he would cook dinner for me once he recovered.

However, weeks later, George confided that it was not the cancer that was killing him but the experimental medication he was taking in hopes of advancing medical research. His selfless participation in a clinical trial ultimately cost him his life—but not in vain.

At his funeral, I reflected on his sacrifice, likening it to the greatest act of love that Jesus spoke of—laying down one's life for others.

Another Loss, Another Test of Faith

Years later, his wife, Linda, called with the devastating news—their son Chris, a successful physician, had been diagnosed with cancer. Chris and his sister, Theresa, both doctors, ran a clinic dedicated to serving their community. As he battled his illness, Chris often found comfort in our conversations. One morning, before I started Mass, he called to thank me for being like an older brother to him, a sentiment that deeply moved me. I promised to call him later, but that time never came.

A few days later, Linda called again, urging me to visit the hospital. Chris was nearing his end and needed the Anointing of the Sick. She then shared something even more heartbreaking—she herself was in another hospital room, preparing for surgery. She couldn't be by her dying son's side, and no words could ease her pain. I reminded her of **Mary at the foot of the cross,** witnessing the suffering of her own son. Though I knew it could not fully console her, I prayed that the God of all comfort would grant her the strength to endure this moment with faith.

At Chris's funeral, I read from the Gospel of John:

"I am the Resurrection and the Life. Whoever believes in me, even though he has died, shall live." (John 11:25)

These words provided a glimmer of hope amid their sorrow. That Christmas, Linda and Theresa invited me to a special dinner, where they shared stories of George and Chris, keeping their memories alive. It was bittersweet but beautiful—a testament to how love and faith endure beyond grief.

A Third Blow: When Faith is Tested to Its Limits

Months later, another heartbreaking call came from Linda—her only remaining family member, Theresa, had been diagnosed with cancer. Despite her strong faith, Linda was overcome with grief, questioning why God would allow such suffering. I had no easy answers.

Theresa's battle mirrored that of her father and brother—treatments, hospital stays, hope, setbacks, and ultimately, the final farewell. At her funeral, Linda stood alone but not abandoned—her friends, neighbors, and parish community surrounded her with love and support.

· · ·

Faith in the Face of Unimaginable Suffering

Through three devastating losses, Linda remained steadfast in faith. Like Job in the Bible, she refused to turn away from God, even as her world crumbled around her.

I was reminded of St. Paul's words:

"I have fought the good fight, I have finished the race, I have kept the faith. Now there is in store for me the crown of righteousness, which the Lord, the righteous Judge, will award to me on that day." (2 Timothy 4:7-8)

Linda fought the good fight, carrying the weight of sorrow with grace and faith. Though brokenhearted, she held onto the hope of reunion in eternity, trusting in the promise of resurrection.

Her story is a reminder that in life's darkest trials, faith does not eliminate suffering—but it gives us the strength to endure it. And in that endurance, God meets us, carries us, and ultimately leads us home.

Chapter 16
Scriptural Perspectives of Aging

In the rich tapestry of Sacred Scripture, the thread of aging is woven with vibrancy. Here, we encounter a diverse array of characters, from those in the bloom of youth to those who have weathered the storms of old age. This diversity underscores the universality of the human journey called aging.

As we delve into this enigma, the inspired texts of the Bible offer us profound insights through their characters and narratives. The theology of aging is firmly grounded here, bathed in the radiance of divine providence. The Bible presents us with a mosaic of stories, insights, and wisdom that illuminate the path of aging with profound meaning and a beacon of hope.

Characters and Messages

From the Psalms, where the poets' reflections echo the sentiments of our own experience, to the Wisdom Literature, where the sages' contemplative statements provide a timeless guide to our encounter with afflictions and mortality, the Bible's wisdom on aging is not just a relic of the past, but a living, ever-relevant guide. Its passages, speaking directly to our hearts, remind us of the importance of seeking wisdom as a guiding light in our aging journey. The sage words of **Proverbs** and the thoughtful reflections of **Ecclesiastes** continue to resonate, offering a reassuring perspective on the vanity of human endeavors.

Then we encounter aging figures such as **Abraham and Sarah**, whose faith-filled journey leads them into the twilight years with unwavering trust in the promises of God. There is **Job,** who voices his grievances to God and even expresses anger at God when he faces the harshest tragedies in life, yet ultimately comes to terms with reality due to his faith and trust in God. We walk alongside **Moses**, whose life serves as a touching reminder of the cyclical nature of life and the legacy that perhaps mirrors our own. We witness the stories of aging patriarchs and matriarchs whose faith and loyalty can inspire us in our twilight years.

At the heart of the life and messages of Biblical characters lies a profound theme of trust in the providence of God. This trust, which accompanies us throughout our earthly pilgrimage, is not just a historical fact but a living reality. It is exemplified in the lives of Elijah, Isaiah, Jeremiah, and Ezekiel, who found strength and solace in God even in their old age. Their stories — along with those of elders like Simeon and Anna, who patiently awaited the coming of the Messiah even in their twilight years — fill our hearts with inspiration and enduring hope, underscoring the living reality of trust in God's plan.

Chapter 17
Prophet Elijah A Prototype

Elijah, a beacon of resilience for the aged, stood firm in the face of adversity and discouragement, never wavering in his faith. His life, chronicled throughout the Bible, is a testament to unwavering godliness and strength.

Elijah makes his first appearance in the **Book of Kings, chapter 17**. It was during King Ahab's reign that he proclaimed a drought as punishment for introducing the cult of Baal in Israel due to his pagan wife Jezebel's influence. Later, Elijah met 450 prophets of Baal in a contest of strength on Mount Carmel to prove who the real God was. When the pagan prophets failed to bring down the fire of the sacrifice they had placed on the altar for Baal, at Elijah's prayers, Yahweh answered by a fire on his altar. The drought ended thereupon with the falling rain. The story is an exciting read. But then comes the twist to the plot.

Elijah's Struggles

Enraged by Elijah's actions, Jezebel sought his life, and he was forced to flee to Mount Horeb (Sinai). Despite his victory over the pagan prophets, the Book of Kings reveals that he was not immune to fear, a human emotion that even the most faithful can experience.

This portrayal of Elijah's human struggles is a powerful reminder that we are not alone in our battles and that even the most steadfast can face moments of fear and uncertainty. Elijah's story is a testament to the shared human experience of struggle and faith.

Despite his moments of isolation and occasional confusion about God's plan, Elijah's unwavering faith was a beacon of light. In return, he was blessed with numerous demonstrations of God's power, such as when he miraculously revived the widow's son, emerged triumphant on Mount Carmel, and called down fire from heaven upon the king's men. These divine interventions remind us of God's presence and strength in Elijah's life. They teach us the profound power of faith and trust in God's plan, inspiring us and reinforcing the importance of trust in God's plan even in the face of adversity.

The narrative of Elijah is not just a story but a source of solace and empowerment for those grappling with unforeseen challenges. It teaches us that unwavering faith in God does not shield us from discouragement but guides us to seek solace in Him in adversity. This narrative is a comforting and strengthening source for all of us.

Chapter 18
Disheartened Like Elijah?

Are you feeling disheartened, reflecting on past triumphs and the vulnerability of old age? Remember, you're not alone in these feelings. Consider the journey of the prophet Elijah, who, despite his triumph on Mt. Carmel, found himself in the depths of depression under a juniper tree. His story resonates with our own struggles, offering a beacon of hope and understanding. Elijah experienced a period of intense fear and depression after a significant victory. Nonetheless, he conquered it all.

Depressed: Many factors can cause depression. Though Elijah's journey started with a fight, it ended in flight, leading to depression. Several factors lead to depression. Let us see how it happened in Elijah's life. In one of his blogs, Dr. Mark Riley, the co-founder and executive director of SoulCare Counseling, gives an impressive insight into Elijah's life situations.[1] Imagine the life of Elijah, a man of faith whose trust in God was once overshadowed by

---

1. "Suffering Depression? So did God's Prophet Elijah" Dr. Mark Riley, co-founder and executive director of SoulCare Counseling

fear. His story is a powerful reminder for us to reflect on the impact of fear in our own lives and how it can lead to feelings of depression and worthlessness..

Afraid: We read in 1 Kings 19:3, "Therefore, Elijah was afraid. And rising up, he went away to wherever his will would carry him." In fact, he was running away in fear. He said to God, "It is enough for me, O Lord. Take my soul." It tells us that fear might lead to depression - fear of not getting the results of a job well done, fear of getting sick, fear of children not doing what they are supposed to do or seeing the tragedies of their lives, the list goes on and on. Look at Elijah for a moment. He went through all these.

Weak: Elijah could not stop Israel's idolatry more than the prophets before him. 1 Kings 19:4 says, "Take my soul. For I am no better than my fathers." When we are gripped by depression, it is typical to blame ourselves and say, "I am practically useless and a failure. I am incompetent even to help my spouse in his/her ill health."

Weary: Depression is always reflected in our physical condition and well-being. In 1 Kings 19:5, we see Elijah emotionally and spiritually exhausted and drained of all energy, sleeping under a juniper tree. When you say, "I don't want to get up from my bed," or "I am not hungry. Leave me alone," or when you refuse to take your medication, you need an angel (as in the case of Elijah, to tell you "Rise up and eat" (1Kings 19:5). Don't just eat and drink and then go back to sleep (1Kings 19:6). The angel will have to remind you again, "Rise up and eat. For a great journey stands before you." (1 Kings 19:7). If you read the rest of chapter 19, you will definitely find great motivation to continue with better motivation and vigor.

Worthless: Have you ever said, "I did so much for my children and family. They got everything they wanted out of me. Now, look, they don't even bother to call me. I brought them up as good Catholics, but they don't even go to Church now." It reflects how Elijah complained to God, "I have been very zealous on behalf of the Lord .... The sons of Israel have forsaken your covenant.... And they are seeking my life." (1 King 19:10) The passage that follows is fantastic - how he was asked to stand waiting for the Lord and how God spoke to him in the whisper of a gentle breeze rather than in the strong wind, earthquake, or fire. Elijah heard it.

When he intently listened to God's voice, his life also changed. That is what we need to do as well. Listen to the Lord in the silence of our hearts. Listening to the Lord is not just a passive act, but a transformative experience. We will not just hear Him speak to us but find hope and direction in His words, guiding us through our own struggles and uncertainties. Listen to God's voice and find a new purpose or task that will motivate us again to shake off the negative thoughts and get active. As Dr. Mark Riley points out, "Sometimes the best way out of depression is to get our focus off of ourselves and onto a new purpose, a new mission."

Feeling weary, depressed, or weak? In the next chapter, we journey into the heart of a touching story about a once-vibrant member of a parish community who faced these very struggles. Despite the hardships, she persevered with unwavering faith in God.

Chapter 19
With God's Help

Diana was a devoted Catholic who was deeply involved in her parish's Women's Guild and tirelessly organized fundraisers. She volunteered at the food pantry and brightened community activities with her bubbly personality. Known for her hospitality, she often welcomed priests to her home for dinner with her husband.

Then came the call that changed everything. Diana phoned to inform me that she had been diagnosed with lung cancer and needed the Anointing of the Sick before surgery. When I visited her at home, I was shocked to notice her pale, frail appearance and the soft wheeze in her voice. Seeing a cheerful and high-spirited woman in such a condition was painful. "Father, you might not know, but I was a chain smoker. When I was growing up, it was cool for young girls to smoke —and eventually, it became a habit," she confessed. I replied gently, "I understand, Diana."

I prayed, read the scripture passage about Jesus healing the sick, and anointed her. I assured her of my ongoing prayers and asked her to update me.

As I prepared to leave, I glanced back and was surprised to see her reaching for a pack of cigarettes. As if reading my thoughts, she offered a sad smile and said, "Does it matter anymore, Father?"

After surgery, the prognosis was grim, and Diana passed away within months. Her journey made me reflect on how difficult it can be to break destructive habits—even when faced with dire consequences. In her life, I saw the enduring spark of her personality, her active participation in parish activities, her deep disappointment in confronting cancer, and, ultimately, her quiet surrender. Yet, throughout it all, Diana's faith never wavered; she found peace in her final days.

I began to wonder how many of us struggle to shed the bad habits we accumulate, even when we know how damaging they can be to our body, mind, and spirit. I recalled Jesus' words in Mark 10:27: **"With man it is impossible, but not with God. For with God, all things are possible."**

Overcoming addiction is a challenging road, but God's grace offers healing for mind, body, and spirit. Never hesitate to ask for His help. As Hebrews 13:5-6 reminds us, "For He has said, 'I will not abandon you, nor will I forsake you.' So we can confidently say, 'The Lord is my helper; I will not be afraid. What can man do to me?'"

Chapter 20
Job In His Later Life

The Book of Job is one of the most acclaimed of the Bible primarily because it explores some of the most profound questions people ask about their lives. The beginning of the book of Job is this: "There was a man in the land of Uz named Job, and he was a simple, honest man, fearing God and withdrawing from evil." (Job 1:1). He was immensely rich and had seven sons and three daughters. The book also says, "This man was great among all the peoples of the east." (Job 1:3)

However, this prosperity did not last. The narrative takes a dramatic turn as Satan appears before God and is granted permission to test Job with afflictions. Stripped of his wealth, his children slain, and his body afflicted, Job finds himself on a heap of ash outside the town. Initially, Job's response to these afflictions shows remarkable faith and submission. He utters, **"The Lord gave, and the Lord has taken away; blessed be the name of the Lord."** However, as his suffering intensifies, Job's faith begins to waver, and he directs his complaints to God, asking, "How many iniquities and sins do I have?... Why do you conceal your face from me?" (Job 3: 23-24)

Job's Wife's Response

Job's wife, who had also endured the same losses as Job, responds to their shared suffering with a stark contrast in attitude. Her cynicism is palpable as she confronts Job with a bitter remark, **"Do you still hold fast to your integrity? Curse God and die."** Her words, filled with disbelief and scorn, question Job's virtue. In the context of the time, it was commonly believed that sickness, death, and tragedy were God's punishment for sins. It is a poignant reminder of the additional burden Job had to bear in the form of his wife's negativity. However, it's important to note that she, too, was suffering, and her response was a reflection of her own pain and confusion.

Job's wife also tells us that when we are hurting, we, too, may easily blame the very ones we love. In your later years, you may also go through unexpected situations you did not plan for. They may be illnesses, death of dear ones, loss of wealth, destruction, or poverty. How will you respond to them? Will you lash out and alienate yourself from your dear ones, or will you draw near to them?

Job's Friends' Views

In their misguided attempts to make sense of his suffering, Job's friends propose a simplistic explanation. They argue that the severity of Job's afflictions must be a sign of his grave sins, and God is punishing him. This reflects a typical, naive understanding of the time. Job, however, is quick to challenge their assumption, asserting that there is no direct correlation between righteousness and prosperity or wickedness and suffering. He makes it clear that he values God more than his wealth, family, and health. Job's response to his friends' misconceptions is significant as it shows his unwavering faith and refusal to accept their limited understanding of God's ways.

Lessons to Learn

The main lesson we learn from Job's suffering is that Satan can shake but cannot destroy someone's faith unless man lets him. Second, sanctification is worth any pain in this life. Man does not see God's wisdom or plan. With the limited human knowledge we have, we question Him. God's questions to Job, from the whirlwind, answer human questions about suffering. God asked Job, **"Where were you when I set the earth's foundations? Tell me, if you understand."** All the questions about the mysteries of the universe God asked Job (Chapter 38) are worth reflecting on when we have questions about human suffering. Despite ignorance of what is happening in the universe, we presume to question God.

At the end of the book, we realize that God understands our sufferings and struggles. He feels our anxieties, worries, and fears. More importantly, He sees our future that we have no clue about. God knows that what we are going through is only temporary, even though, at that moment, it may be intensely crushing. Though Job felt the same way in his struggles, he never lost sight of God. Job did not curse God and go away. He debated with God but listened to what God had to say. The book of Job ends with the positive note that God blessed him with twice what he had before.

Finally, Job submitted himself to God's wisdom and goodness. He confessed, "I have been speaking foolishly, about things whose measure exceeds my knowledge" (Job 42: 3). We will arrive at that realization once we acknowledge that we are not in control. There is someone in control whose knowledge and wisdom are infinite—God.

In Conclusion

When you look back on the achievements of your life and the power and glory you had enjoyed, it may be hard to reckon with the helplessness you might experience in later years. The realization Job arrived at after all the suffering and mental agony is what you should have when encountering trials related to aging. Make up your mind to accept the reality of life and find happiness in the present rather than dwelling on the glories of the past and feeling miserable. Trust in God enough to have the hope to look beyond the darkness of the night to the brightness of the morning.

Chapter 21
Inspiration from Biblical Characters

O ur faith and hope in God do not eliminate all problems. Instead, they empower us with the inner strength and conviction to face them and to keep ourselves sane even when the storms of life buffet our lives' ship.

Take time to read those passages in the Bible, such as [**Psalm 71:9, 18; Isaiah 46:4; 2 Corinthians 4:16**], which speak about the enduring nature of God's love and the promise of renewal even in old age. Read a chapter at a time, and take a few moments to reflect on it. See how those stories and insights shape your understanding of the aging process. Are there similarities? How do you handle such situations? When we look closely at the lives of these characters, we see that **we** can draw strength and inspiration from the faith and wisdom of our spiritual ancestors as we struggle through the challenges and opportunities of our later years.

Biblical characters, with their unwavering trust in God and relentless pursuit of His will, showcase a resilience and faithfulness that can serve as a guiding light in our aging journey. As we delve into their stories and reflect on their wisdom, we can gain insights that reshape our understanding of aging in the modern world, reminding us of every individual's inherent dignity and value.

In a world that often prioritizes youth and productivity, biblical stories offer a counter-cultural message of honor, respect, and reverence for elders. By embracing this biblical perspective on aging, we can strive to create communities that uphold the dignity and worth of older adults, appreciating their wisdom, experience, and valuable contributions to the Church and community. Organizing group gatherings where these stories are shared among older adults and with the parish youth can be a meaningful way to foster this appreciation.

The stories of our ancient ancestors of biblical times serve as a powerful reminder of the resilience, faithfulness, trusting faith, and enduring hope we should maintain through the journey of later life. The stories of the Apostles, especially those narrated in **the Acts of the Apostles and St. Paul's letters**, bear witness to the transformative power of faith and courage in the face of adversity and old age. Consider reading and meditating on them and then sharing your insights in support group meetings, by discussing the lessons learned, relating the stories to personal experiences, or applying the teachings to current challenges.

Simeon and Anna, two elderly figures in the Bible, invite us to view aging as a season of life filled with meaning, purpose, and opportunity for blessings rather than a period of decline or diminishment. Their stories, found in [Luke 2:22-38], illustrate the wisdom and faithfulness that can be found in later life. Simeon's patient waiting for the Messiah and Anna's faithful service in the temple, despite her advanced age, are powerful examples of how aging can be a time of spiritual growth and fulfillment. Reflecting on these stories can help to cultivate a more profound sense of satisfaction and spiritual vitality in later life.

Jesus Christ

Most important of all biblical characters, even more, at the very heart of the Bible, is Jesus Christ. The whole Bible is centered around Him, and His story is the Salvation History. When considering human suffering, there is nothing that comes even close to what Jesus experienced from the garden of Gethsemane to his crucifixion on Calvary. Jesus could have chosen another path as the Son of God, but He obediently did the Father's Will for humanity's salvation. Remember how Jesus prayed, "Father, if you are willing, take this chalice away from me. Yet, truly, let not my will, but yours be done." (Luke 22: 42)

Whatever sufferings we may have, we can always surrender them to God. Remember that God will never abandon us, especially when we suffer in old age. Struggles will always be part of the human journey. It isn't easy to understand why all these challenges happen to us. That is when we look up to Jesus and ask, "Why did He suffer?"

In Conclusion

The Bible showcases different characters who persevered through struggles yet glorified God. These stories inspire us to find meaning in our struggles and, most importantly, strengthen our faith and trust in God. Remember that our struggles are not in vain; they can lead us to a deeper understanding of God's love and grace.

The biblical perspective on aging unfolds a rich tapestry of stories, insights, and wisdom that brighten the days of later life with depth and resonance. As the pages of the Scriptures help us draw inspiration from the faithfulness of those who have gone before us, they will illuminate the path of our journey of aging with hope, courage, and steadfast trust in the providence of God.

In the upcoming chapter, you will encounter a heartwarming real-life story that showcases the profound courage of a woman confronting her impending death. As she navigates this poignant journey, she draws insight and inspiration from a wealth of spiritual resources. This journey transforms her perspective on life, death, and what lies beyond, preparing her for the inevitable with a serene acceptance. Her story offers a deeply moving and refreshing approach to the end of life, inviting us to rethink our views on this natural part of existence.

Chapter 22
From Trusting Faith To Hope
(A sequel to the story in chapter 4)

After the death of her husband, George, Joan Slider experienced profound grief and an overwhelming sense of loss. Yet, in time, she gradually reconnected with family and friends, finding comfort in their company. Determined to live fully despite her sorrow, she resumed her involvement in Church ministries, discovering a renewed sense of purpose and peace.

A few years later, Joan awoke one morning with a strange sensation in her head. Dizziness overwhelmed her, and she collapsed, experiencing a seizure. It felt as though she were caught in a storm, unable to move or cry for help. When she regained consciousness, excruciating pain radiated inside her head. At the hospital, doctors diagnosed her with brain cancer. They informed her that surgery would likely be ineffective, offering only medication to alleviate pain and extend her time.

Shocked and seeking guidance, Joan reached out to me with pressing questions about suffering, eternal life, and preparing for the end of life. She asked whether it was morally acceptable to forgo surgery, and I reassured her that it was. She also sought spiritual direction in ensuring her soul was ready for heaven. These were heart-wrenching questions, ones that many people eventually face.

I encouraged Joan to begin by receiving the Sacraments of Healing, a source of great peace for the soul. She made her Confession, experiencing the grace of forgiveness and reconciliation, followed by the Anointing of the Sick, which provides spiritual strength in illness and suffering. These sacred moments brought her deep comfort as she entrusted herself more fully into God's hands.

As the weeks passed, Joan became increasingly tired, and her daughter moved in to care for her. During my visits, they often shared stories and meals, creating a sense of normalcy amidst the illness. These simple moments—filled with laughter, conversation, and the warmth of companionship—became a source of strength for Joan.

Six months later, Joan called with a special request: she wanted to receive the Sacrament of Healing one last time, followed by dinner at a neighborhood restaurant. When I arrived, she shared the painful reality—her headaches and seizures had worsened, and her doctors believed her final days were near. She wanted to be anointed and receive the Eucharist, Viaticum, meaning "food for the journey."

I read to her from the Letter of St. James about the Anointing of the Sick:

"Is anyone among you sick? Let them call the elders of the church to pray over them and anoint them with oil in the name of the Lord. And the prayer offered in faith will make the sick person well; the Lord will raise them up." (James 5:14-15)

After praying, I anointed her and gave her Holy Communion, which she received with a look of quiet gratitude.

Then, despite her frailty, Joan insisted on our dinner outing. Though visibly weak, she chatted enthusiastically, her eyes sparkling with an energy that seemed almost beyond her physical limitations. It was as if she were preparing for a long-awaited journey, one she faced with acceptance and trust in God's promises.

As we returned to her home, she hugged warmly, offering a

goodbye that felt profoundly final. As I left, I had a strong feeling this was the last time I would see her alive.

A week later, her daughter called to inform me that Joan had entered hospice care. When I visited, she lay unconscious, wrapped in a serene stillness. I prayed with her and her daughter, offering a final blessing, sensing that she was at the threshold of eternity. The next day, I received the news of Joan's passing.

Reflecting on Joan's journey, I found consolation in the knowledge that she had faced death not with fear, but with deep faith and spiritual preparedness. In her final months, she taught those around her what it means to trust in God until the very end.

Jesus' words echoed in my heart:

"I am the Resurrection and the Life. Whoever believes in me, even though he has died, shall live." (John 11:25)

Joan's story is a testament to the power of faith and the hope it brings, reminding us all that as we age and face life's final chapter, God's grace is sufficient, and His promises are certain.

Chapter 23
Mortality A Reality

The ultimate reality of human existence centers around the inevitability of death and the mystery of what lies beyond. As we navigate the vast sea of mortality, we have no choice but to confront the fears that surround the uncertainties of what lies beyond death. However, let's take a deep and logical look into the purpose of life. In this exploration, we will find solace in the eternal promise of life, a comforting and hopeful understanding of our mortality that reassures us.

Embracing the reality of mortality is a crucial starting point in our philosophical journey. It sets the stage for exploring life's ultimate questions and helps us understand the necessity of confronting our fears and anxieties surrounding death.

Afraid of Mortality?

Though ordinary people are afraid to think of mortality, we must start by acknowledging its reality. Whether we like it or not, all creatures that come into existence have to face death. The inevitability of death is woven into the fabric of life. Therefore, before everything else, we should confront our fears and anxieties surrounding the reality of our mortality. This is not a choice but a necessity to have the freedom to live fully and authentically in the present moment, empowering us and giving us a sense of control.

Once we confront and come to terms with the inevitability of the end of our lives, the next step is to gain an understanding of what happens after death. There is no logical human explanation other than saying that once we die, our body disintegrates, just like that of any living creature. Is that all there is to human life after all your outstanding achievements? Are we just bodies that disintegrate and turn out to be nothing but dust?

Even in human terms, we say that we are a composite of matter and spirit (body and mind). The 'spirit' here refers to the non-physical aspect of our being, which includes our consciousness, emotions, and personality. Matter will die and disintegrate, but this 'spirit' doesn't. The qualities of our spiritual existence are intelligence, which helps us achieve all the great things in our lives, and free will, which allows us to make decisions and follow them up firmly. It doesn't die with the body, which is matter.

If our spirit doesn't die with the body, it has to go somewhere when the body dies. But where? Human intelligence cannot answer that question. Neither can science because science deals with physical realities, not the spiritual. Therefore, we must look to theology, which deals with spiritual truths, for a rational explanation. Drawing on the wisdom of Sacred Scripture and spiritual traditions and experience, we can explore the profound mystery of death and the transformative power of faith in the face of mortality, offering a sense of hope and comfort.

The Next Chapter presents the inspiring testimony of an individual who encountered Christ in the Sacraments in the final days of his life. His unwavering faith led him on a profound journey to meet his Creator face-to-face. As he reflected on his journey, every step seemed to have led him to a moment of peaceful surrender, where hope and fulfillment intertwined, preparing his soul for the final, divine embrace.

Chapter 24
No Real Goodbyes

J oe Reamer joined our parish's RCIA (Rite of Christian Initiation for Adults) program with a fervent desire to become Catholic. Despite severe health issues, he diligently attended every class, absorbing Church teachings and asking thoughtful, insightful questions about Catholic doctrine and discussed them with his classmates who sought him out. His wife, Sue, a devout Catholic, supported him wholeheartedly in his faith journey.

Halfway through the year-long course, Joe received devastating news—he had been diagnosed with cancer. Yet, despite his illness, he remained unwavering in his commitment, continuing to attend as many classes as his strength allowed. Even as Joe underwent chemotherapy, his determination never wavered. However, as his condition worsened, he could no longer participate. When treatments proved ineffective, Joe and Sue made the painful decision to cease all medication. His health declined rapidly.

A Request from the Heart

I visited Joe often, praying with him and offering comfort, but I could not yet administer the Sacrament of the Anointing of the Sick, as he was not yet Catholic.

As I prepared to leave one afternoon, Joe, his voice filled with emotion, hesitantly asked, "Father, can I receive Baptism?" He continued, "I know I haven't completed the course. But I believe in Jesus, and know enough about the Catholic faith to receive Baptism. Will you please consider?"

His faith moved me deeply. Here was a man on the threshold of eternity, longing to fully embrace Christ and His Church. I looked at him and said, "Joe, I think you are ready for Baptism. Talk to Sue, and let me know when you'd like to receive it."

A few days later, Sue called to set a date. Accompanied by our RCIA coordinator, I visited their home to baptize Joe. It was a deeply sacred moment—a man facing death, yet filled with peace, eager to become a child of God through water and the Spirit. As I poured the blessed water over him, I saw his profound faith and trust in God. This Baptism was not just a ritual but a true transformation—a final step in his earthly journey toward heaven.

Final Steps of Faith

Within a month, Joe's condition deteriorated further, and he was admitted into hospice care.

Sue asked again, "Father, now that Joe is baptized, can he receive the Anointing of the Sick?" Without hesitation, I agreed. This sacrament, meant to bring spiritual healing and grace in the face of suffering, was now open to him.

As I was about to leave, Joe had one more request—his voice, though weak, was filled with longing:

"Father, can I receive the Eucharist? I want to receive Jesus at least once before I die."

Overwhelmed by the depth of his faith, I immediately returned with the Eucharist, the real presence of Christ.

After making his first confession, Joe received Holy Communion with profound reverence and devotion. This was his first and only Communion, but it was also his Viaticum—the "Food for the Journey." He was spiritually prepared to meet God, with Christ now dwelling in him.

No Real Goodbyes

The next day, Joe passed away. His journey on earth had ended, but his journey with Christ had only begun.

As I reflected on his faith and perseverance, Jesus' words in the Beatitudes came to mind:

"Blessed are the pure of heart, for they shall see God." (Matthew 5:8)

Joe's profound faith, unwavering devotion, and the desire to fully unite with Christ made his final days a testament to God's grace and love.

Instead of saying "Goodbye" to Joe, I found myself whispering, "See you, Joe."

Chapter 25
Spiritual Dimensions of Aging

The first realization when we consider the spiritual dimensions of death is that it is not an end but a threshold or gateway to a new life and eternal communion with the supreme spiritual being - God. In most world religions, death is viewed not as the final chapter but as a transition to a new form of existence. This perspective invites us to view death as a passage through which we move from our earthly life to a deeper union with the divine power that gave us this existence. It should be called a sacred threshold where the temporal gives way to the eternal, and the finite merges with the infinite.

The Transformative Power of Faith

When confronted with mortality, faith becomes our guiding light, offering a comforting framework to comprehend death. It provides strength in the face of the unknown, transforming our fear of death into acceptance of the natural order of human existence. Faith instills trust in the divine promise of eternal life, nurturing this transformative power through reading sacred texts, prayer, meditation, and community support. Understanding the meaning of death and the afterlife can help individuals and families find peace and comfort as they confront death.

Hope in the Promise of Resurrection

As we journey through the shadowlands of mortality, we find hope in the promise of Resurrection. It assures us that death does not have the final word and that life triumphs over death in the eternal embrace of divine love. We draw inspiration from the stories of saints and mystics who have journeyed to the threshold of death and returned with messages of hope, healing, and redemption. This promise of Resurrection instills in us a sense of hope and anticipation for what lies beyond.

Faced with mortality, we encounter the ultimate mystery of human experience—the mystery of life's fragile beauty and eternal promise. This mystery, often referred to as the 'mystery of life and death,' is a profound and awe-inspiring aspect of our spiritual journey. Hence, our reflections on death and dying should be guided by a deep sense of reverence, gratitude, and awe for the gift of life. We find confidence in the assurance that in death, as in life, we are held in the tender embrace of God's love.

Embracing Death with Hope and Grace

Ultimately, facing mortality means embracing the full spectrum of life, including the final moment. This 'full spectrum of life' encompasses all the joys, sorrows, challenges, and triumphs that we experience. By preparing spiritually and emotionally, we can face death not with fear but with a sense of accomplishment, gratitude, serene tranquility, and hope. The Christian promise of Resurrection assures us that death is not a final 'goodbye' but a 'see you later' as we transition into the newness of life in the presence of God.

Tailpiece

A man who had been a notorious criminal most of his life was in the hospital for surgery. Coming out from under the anesthetic, he saw that the blinds to the hospital room were drawn. He complained to the nurse that he could not see out and asked why they were drawn. The nurse replied, "Calm down. There is a big fire burning everything across the street. We didn't want you to wake up and think that the operation failed."

Chapter 26
Death in World Religions

In exploring the theology of aging, we encounter a universal human experience - contemplating death. While death may stir fear and sorrow, it also carries a profound spiritual significance that transcends religious boundaries, uniting us in a shared understanding of life's ultimate transition. From a spiritual standpoint, death is not the end but a transition to a new form of existence, inviting us to see it as a gateway from earthly life to a deeper union with the divine. This perspective resonates across various religious and spiritual traditions, each offering unique teachings on the mystery and meaning of death.

Hinduism: According to Hinduism, humans transition through a process called reincarnation. It means each person's soul ("Atman" in Sanskrit) passes through a long cycle of existence, occupying different bodies through repeated births, deaths, and rebirths. Their sacred book, 'Bhagavad Gita,' teaches that the soul (Atman) is eternal, and at death, it is just the shedding of the body.

The soul of the deceased enters the body of another species of creation, depending on their life in this life. If a person's "Karma" or actions are not meritorious, the soul will reincarnate as a lower caste person or through an animal's body. Karma refers to the law of cause and effect. It means one's actions in this life determine the circumstances in the next.

This cycle continues until finally, the soul reunites with God or the universal Soul ("Brahman"). It is 'Nirvana' or 'Moksha,' the highest level of existence that does not have the suffering of earthly life. Essentially, it means that the soul rejoins the supreme energy that created the universe.

Buddhism: Buddhism originated from Hinduism and shares some similarities with its predecessor. The supreme aim of Buddhism is to attain **'Nirvana,'** or enlightenment, a state of liberation from the cycles of birth, death, and rebirth through countless lives up and down the six states of existence. Mindfulness or meditation prepares individuals to face death, and there is no reward or punishment after death. This perspective on death and rebirth is a key principle of Buddhism.

Judaism: The most important Jewish book, "The Torah," does not explicitly reference the afterlife. The dead go to **"Sheol,"** a kind of Hades, where they live in an ethereal, shadowy existence. (Num. 16:13 and Ps. 6:6). Talmudic rabbis believe there were allusions to it in the Bible, in the **Book of Daniel**. It also holds that many of those who sleep in the dust of the earth shall awake, some to everlasting life and some to everlasting abhorrence. (Isaiah 26:19 and Ezekiel 37: 1) Some hold that the resurrection of the dead will follow the messianic era. However, in general, Judaism is ambiguous about this matter of heaven and hell.

Christianity: In Christianity, death is often understood in the context of Jesus Christ's resurrection, a promise of eternal life for believers. This theological concept of resurrection is a central pillar of the Christian faith, and numerous New Testament passages provide clear insights into death and resurrection.

The Christian perspective on death and resurrection is rooted in the life and teachings of Jesus Christ. It offers profound comfort and reassurance, making it a beacon of hope among all world religions.

Catholic rituals, such as the Sacrament of the Anointing of the Sick, prayers for the dying, and funeral liturgy, underscore faith in resurrection and hope in eternal life.

Chapter 27
Be Prepared for the Inevitable

P reparing for the end of life is a deeply spiritual and
emotional journey that offers us the chance to nurture and
deepen our relationship with God. The transformative
power of forgiveness and reconciliation is paramount in this journey.
Despite the difficulty of forgiving grave offenses, even those
committed by our own family, it is crucial to release those burdens
and extend a hand in reconciliation. We can find healing and inner
peace by addressing unresolved conflicts, seeking forgiveness, and
offering our own. The Sacrament of Reconciliation, with its confession and absolution, provides a sense of spiritual cleansing and
renewal. Similarly, the Sacrament of Anointing of the Sick offers
forgiveness of sins and spiritual healing.

Reflecting on Life's Journey

We begin by reflecting on the journey of our life that has brought
us to the present moment with its triumphs and tribulations, joys and
sorrows, struggles and challenges, milestones and memories that have
shaped our lives and forged our identity. We see the tapestry of our
lives woven with the threads of meaning and purpose that offer us
guidance and direction as we navigate the twilight years.

Engaging in Lifelong Growth

Next, we divert our attention to the unique gifts and blessings of aging, such as wisdom tempered with experience, expertise gained and sharpened by years of work, and insight developed over the years by understanding human nature and behavior. These can help us offer our service to family or community members. For instance, you can share your professional expertise with younger generations or volunteer at a local charity. Further, we get the freedom to explore new passions and interests. This could be learning a new language, taking up a new hobby, or even starting a new career.

As we journey through the twilight years, we can discover new avenues of learning and growth that nurture a fresh sense of meaning and purpose. This often involves exploring new paths of fulfillment and contribution. Retirement is not the end but the beginning of a new chapter where our personal passions and long-cherished interests can thrive. Whether it's continuing education in our field of interest or deepening our spiritual understanding, these pursuits are not mere hobbies. They can unlock a more profound sense of purpose and fulfillment in our later years.

This phase of life is a time of freedom and empowerment. It allows us to engage in activities that bring joy and satisfaction, such as volunteering, mentoring, and pursuing hobbies previously sidelined by career and family responsibilities. Embrace the possibilities before us, and look forward to the exciting renewal opportunities each day. This sense of freedom and the myriad of opportunities can empower us and fill us with optimism as we navigate the later stages of life.

Challenges Can Also Be Opportunities

While finding purpose in later years can be rewarding, it also presents challenges. Health issues, the loss of loved ones, and societal attitudes towards aging can be significant obstacles. However, these challenges are manageable. They can be redefined as opportunities for growth and resilience. We can engage in deeper introspection and renew our sense of purpose. Adopting a proactive and positive mindset, seeking spiritual guidance, and maintaining social connections can provide us with the strength and resilience we need to overcome these challenges.

Tailpiece

An elderly couple visited a tech store to check out the latest smartwatch. After a quick demo, the salesman asked, "Well, what do you say?"

The husband asked, "Will it remind us when it's time for our afternoon nap?"

With a smile, the salesman said, "We can program it to do just that!"

The wife said, "Wow! Finally, a gadget that understands our priorities!"

Chapter 28
Finding Purpose in Later Life

How do we find and sustain a sense of purpose in later life? This question, deeply rooted in theological insights and practical wisdom, has the transformative power to shape our vision and enrich our lives as we age. As we navigate the complexities of aging, we should uncover the deep reservoirs of wisdom, resilience, and grace within us. This exploration of purpose, inspired by theological insights, will undoubtedly inspire and motivate us, illuminating the path ahead with purpose and significance.

Theological Foundations of Purpose

From a theological perspective, our sense of purpose is deeply intertwined with our faith and spiritual convictions. In the Christian tradition, death holds profound theological significance. It is not seen as an end but rather as a transition to eternal life with God.

This concept of 'eternal life with God' refers to a state of being in which we are in a close, eternal relationship with God, experiencing his love, joy, and peace in a way that is beyond our current understanding. It is a life free from the limitations and struggles of our earthly existence, where we are fully united with God and experience his divine presence in its fullness. This eternal life is not just a continuation of our current life, but a state of being that transcends time and space, where we are in perfect harmony with God and all creation.

Everything that happens with our bodies in later years reminds us that we are not created for this world. If we look logically at what happens to us physically and mentally, we notice that we are slowly fading into that moment of our spirit separating from the feeble body.

At this time, Jesus Christ's resurrection assures us of the promise of life beyond death and provides us with a profound sense of hope and comfort. This belief, the cornerstone of the Christian faith, transforms our understanding of death as a gateway to a new and everlasting existence with God. This theological perspective offers a reassuring and optimistic outlook on aging and purpose, instilling a sense of peace and serenity.

The Redemptive Value of Suffering

Suffering is an inevitable part of life, especially in old age. Christianity teaches that suffering and death have a redemptive value. This means that **our physical, psychological, or spiritual suffering, when united with the suffering of Jesus, can serve a purpose** beyond our immediate understanding. The term 'redemptive value of suffering' refers to the belief that our suffering, when offered up to God in union with the suffering of Jesus, can contribute to the redemption of humanity.

In simpler terms, our suffering, when united with Jesus' suffering, can be a source of healing and transformation for ourselves and others. This is not to say that suffering is inherently good, but that it can be transformed into something meaningful and redemptive when united with the suffering of Jesus. His sacrifice was not for Himself, nor was it a random event. It was part of a divine plan for the salvation of humanity.

This gratuitous suffering tells us there is a value to our suffering, too, if seen from the proper perspective. This perspective can provide a profound sense of dignity and purpose, even in the face of our pain and loss, instilling a sense of worth and significance that transcends our earthly struggles, offering comfort and reassurance.

The Communion of Saints

In our chapter about the Scriptural perspective on aging, we saw that the Bible abounds with stories of picturesque characters who found purpose in their later years. These include figures like **Moses,** who led the Israelites out of Egypt in his old age, and **Anna,** the prophetess who recognized the baby Jesus as the Messiah in her old age. These astounding stories illustrate how God calls us to meaningful service at every stage of life. This service can take many forms, from leadership and prophecy to acts of kindness and compassion.

The biblical expression 'gathered to his people' is an ancient way of referring to death, as seen in the description of **Abraham's death**: 'And declining, he died at a good old age, and at an advanced stage of life, and full of days. And he was "gathered to his people." (Genesis 25:8) These stories are powerful examples of how we can find and fulfill our purpose in later life, even in the face of challenges and limitations.

Gathered to his people in the Bible refers to the dead joining past generations who have died. Biblically, it also refers to the gathering of the spirits of the dead in one place in the afterlife. That place is heaven. The consistent teaching of Scripture is that there is life after death: "The dust returns to its earth, from which it was, and the spirit returns to God who granted it." (Ecclesiastes 12:7). This truth is implied in the Hebrew expression gathered to his people. That expression clarifies the Christian teaching of 'Communion of Saints.'

The Communion of Saints is a belief in the Christian faith that emphasizes the continuity of our relationship with the loved ones who have passed. It teaches that we remain united with them in the mystical body of Christ, offering a comforting sense of continuity and Communion. This belief includes all who are part of the Christian community: those who are living, those who have passed and are in heaven, and those who are in the process of purification in purgatory. In death, we join those gathered to our people.

Therefore, it is meaningful to pray for those in purgatory and encourage the younger generation to pray for them, especially by offering Mass, the sacramental re-enactment of the paschal mysteries of Jesus' suffering, death, and resurrection. The Communion of Saints assures us that our relationship with our loved ones do not end with death but continues in a spiritual sense. It also reminds us that we are part of a larger community of faith where we can find support, comfort, and hope in times of loss.

Chapter 29
Eschatological Perspective

For people of faith, earthly life is a journey to another life that transcends the limitations of time and space, leading into the boundless immensity of eternity. As we navigate the complexities of aging, we rightly discover that this hope is not merely a feeling but a steadfast anchor for the soul, grounding us in the assurance of life's ultimate promise. **The Christian eschatological doctrine of hope and resurrection, a profound source of comfort and strength**, especially as people approach the twilight years of their lives, provides a reassuring and peaceful understanding of life's ultimate journey. Eschatology is the branch of theology that deals with the end things, such as death, judgment, and the final destiny of the soul and humankind. With its promise of eternal life and resurrection, this doctrine is a beacon of peace and tranquility in the face of life's uncertainties.

The Christian Hope of Eternal Life

At the heart of the Christian faith lies the assurance of eternal life, a hope that is not wishful thinking but a logical realization grounded in the resurrection of Jesus Christ. His resurrection, the cornerstone of our faith, is not just a historical event but a living reality that affirms that death is not the end but a door to eternity. Our faith and hope in the resurrection, a beacon of optimism and upliftment, are not based on mere words but on what Jesus said and did during his earthly life. This logical realization of our hope in eternal life should fill us with a sense of security and confidence in our faith.

John 11: 25-26: Here we see the most significant revelation of Jesus, who said to Martha and Mary as they were grieving the death of their brother Lazarus, "I am the Resurrection and the Life. Whoever believes in me, even though he has died, he shall live."

John 14: 1-6: This text gives us Jesus' assurance of what happens after death. The disciples were distressed when Jesus revealed to them that he would be handed over to be killed, and then, after three days, he would rise. (Mt. 17:22-23) The part about rising did not make any sense to them. So, they were profoundly troubled by the news of His death. In this situation, Jesus tells them, "Do not let your hearts be troubled..... In my Father's house, there are many dwelling places.... **I am going to prepare a place for you**. And if I go and prepare a place for you, I will return, and then I will take you to myself so that where I am, you also may be." It is a clear statement from Jesus about eternal life.

1 Corinthians 15: The Apostle Paul's discourse on the resurrection, a comprehensive theological basis for our hope in eternal life, provides us with a sense of security and hope. Paul reiterates the promise of eternal life and resurrection, stating that just as Christ was raised from the dead, so too will all be brought to life. He asserts that Christ is the first fruits of those who sleep, a testament to the promise of eternal life and resurrection. This powerful affirmation of our hope in eternal life and resurrection in Paul's discourse should inspire us and fill us with hope, knowing that our faith is firmly grounded in a comprehensive theological basis.

Jesus Raising the Dead: As proof for his followers, Jesus raised three people from the dead. First, Jesus raised the daughter of Jairus, the synagogue official, which is recorded in the Synoptic

Gospels. If anyone had doubts about whether she was really dead, Jesus raised the son of a widow of Nain in the funeral procession. (Luke 7:11-17) Still, if someone is skeptical, Jesus raises Lazarus four days after his death. (John 11:38-44). To confirm the fact beyond doubt, Luke reports what Martha had said, "Lord, by now it will smell, for this is the fourth day." However, we should know that Jesus did these miracles not to give them eternal life in this world, for none of them are alive now. It was to show that Jesus had power over sin and death.

Eschatological Dimension of Aging

For people who have no faith, aging is merely a biological process. If we agree with that position, there will be no answer to several human predicaments, such as suffering and injustice, as well as our actions undertaken with our intelligence and free will. Moreover, there is no human answer to the question of where our spiritual component of existence goes when the body dies. Therefore, aging is a process imbued with eschatological significance. The ultimate fulfillment of God's promises brings hope and meaning to our struggles and challenges, especially aging.

Chapter 30
Worried about Salvation?

Richard Coleman, a retired U.S. Army veteran, dedicated his life to service—both to his country and his community. After 27 years in the Army Reserves, he became an active member of St. Michael's Church in Fernandina Beach, where his faith found new expressions in service.

As a devout Catholic, Richard served as an Extraordinary Minister of Holy Communion, bringing the Eucharist to the homebound and hospitalized. He also led a team of volunteers running a cold night shelter for the homeless, ensuring that those in need had a place of refuge during the harshest nights. His unwavering commitment to the poor and vulnerable earned him the Volunteer of the Year award from the Coalition for the Homeless. Yet, he never sought recognition—he did everything in the spirit of Jesus' words:

"Do not let your left hand know what your right hand is doing." (Matthew 6:3)

A Life of Service Rooted in Love
Richard's devotion extended beyond the Church into his

personal life. He lovingly cared for his wife through her prolonged illness, standing by her side until she passed away. His children, shaped by his example, became successful individuals.

I first met Richard when he requested the Sacraments for his ailing wife. Over time, I deeply admired his humility, dedication, and unwavering faith. He gave without seeking acknowledgment, embodying true Christian charity.

However, years of relentless service took a toll on his health. His condition gradually declined, leading to multiple hospital visits and, eventually, a move to an assisted living facility. His children remained devoted throughout this time, ensuring he was never alone. Their love and care spoke volumes about the kind of father Richard had been—a man whose life of faith shaped not just his own destiny but the hearts of those around him.

A Final Concern: The Question of Salvation

Even the most righteous souls may experience moments of doubt when facing the mystery of eternity. One day, his daughter called me from the nursing home, her voice heavy with emotion.

"Father, Dad's condition is worsening. He wants to talk to you."

I hurried to Richard's side, grasping his frail hand. His eyes searched mine, filled with concern.

He hesitantly asked, "Father... what if I don't make it to heaven?"

That question surprised me. How could a man who had lived such a faithful life doubt his own salvation?

I leaned in and spoke to him gently:

"Richard, it is not our merits that save us—it is God's infinite mercy."

I reminded him of his life of faith, his service, and the grace of the Sacraments he had received throughout his life. I spoke of St. Mother Teresa, who had endured years of spiritual darkness near the end of her life. Even great saints have wrestled with doubt, yet God's mercy remains steadfast.

Then, smiling, I added, "Richard, if you don't make it to heaven, people like me have no chance at all."

His worried expression softened, and a small chuckle escaped him.

With that, I administered the Anointing of the Sick for the last time, entrusting him again to the Lord's care.

Welcomed Home

Not too long after that, Richard passed away. In my heart, I imagined Jesus waiting for him, arms open, saying:

"Come, you blessed of my Father. Inherit the kingdom prepared for you from the foundation of the world." (Matthew 25:34)

His life had been one of service, humility, and unwavering faith. His final moments were not filled with fear but with the peace of knowing that God's mercy is greater than our doubts.

For those who fear for their salvation, Richard's story reminds them that it is not our perfection that matters; instead, our trust in God's love. Even in our doubts, God is waiting to welcome us home.

Chapter 31
Comfort Of God's Presence

F aith teaches us that God is with us in every stage of our life, from childhood to our final days. This presence we experience in various ways. In **John 14: 15-31**, we see Jesus promising the **indwelling of the Holy Spirit**. It says, "I will ask the Father, and He will give another Advocate to you, so that He may abide with you for eternity: the Spirit of truth...He will remain with you, and He will be in you." (Jn. 14: 16-17) The Spirit provides continuous guidance, comfort, strength, and courage. Romans 8:11 reminds us that the same Spirit that raised Jesus from the dead lives within us and animates our mortal bodies.

Before He ascended into heaven, Jesus told His disciples, "Teach them to observe all that I have ever commanded you. And behold, I am with you always, even to the consummation of the age" (Mt. 28: 20). **Psalm 23 and Psalm 46** offer comforting assurance of God's presence and protection. The assurance of God's presence and love offers immense comfort and strength.

. . .

In the context of aging, eschatology emphasizes the ultimate fulfillment of God's promises of the life to come. God revealed it perfectly through Jesus Christ, whose resurrection proved everything He had said. That is why St. Paul said, **"What is sown in corruption shall rise to incorruption."** (1Cor. 15:42) and "This corruptibility must be clothed with incorruptibility and for this mortality to be clothed with immortality" (1 Cor. 15:53). This perspective offers a framework to understand our earthly journey as part of a larger plan of God.

Fulfillment of God's Promises

As we delve deeper into the Church's doctrine rooted in biblical revelation, we see that the eschatological perspective assures us that our lives are progressing toward the culmination of a divine plan. Revelation 21:1-4 speaks of the vision of a new heaven and a new earth, where God will dwell with His people, and there will be no more death, mourning, or pain. This vision provides the hope that all creation will be renewed and perfected.

Practical Tips

Looking at life in the light of the promises of Jesus will transform how we approach aging and mortality.

Therefore,

1. **Nurture a sense of deep gratitude** and an insight to recognize each day as a gift and blessing.
2. Learn to **appreciate the present** while looking forward to the future with hope.
3. **Deepen your faith** through spiritual practices that help us trust in God's promises. Regular participation in

the sacraments, prayer, and scripture study reinforce our hope, leaving behind fear and anxiety.

4. **Engage in acts of charity** and service, showing gratitude to God for His blessings. These bring joy and fulfillment and bear witness to the transformative power of God's love.

In Conclusion

Christian hope in the resurrection and eternal life provides an amazing sense of encouragement and strength as we face aging and mortality. By seeing the eschatological dimension of aging, we realize that our lives are part of God's unfolding plan, moving toward the ultimate fulfillment of His promises. The comforting assurance of God's abiding presence and love in every stage of our life offers us peace and joy. It enables us to live with hope amidst the struggles and challenges of later years. Our hope and anticipation of the life to come anchor our souls on solid ground and guide us on the right path toward the eternal embrace of our loving Creator.

Chapter 32
Spiritual Connection

Aging provides an unparalleled opportunity for spiritual growth. As the distractions of our young and career years fade, we can focus more deeply on our relationship with God. The later years can be a time for earnest spiritual renewal when we seek and find a deeper intimacy with the divine. Deepening our connection with God infuses every aspect of our lives with meaning, purpose, and grace.

Through reflection and contemplation, we can better understand our purpose in life and destiny within God's grand design. Prayer, meditation, reading the Bible, and receiving sacraments will nourish our souls and sustain us, rooted in God's grace. To speak in human terms, when we finally arrive in God's presence, we will not be strangers to Him.

Cultivate a Spirituality of Aging

If we want to embrace the spirituality of aging, we should intentionally cultivate practices and attitudes that enhance a deeper intimacy with God and others. Here are some practical tips:

Prayer and Meditation

- **Engage in daily prayer and meditation** to connect with God. These practices provide a sense of peace and grounding and help us face the challenges of aging with a calm spirit. Recalling our daily blessings will reinforce a positive outlook and help foster gratefulness. Reflect on past experiences, recognizing how they have shaped us and contributed to our growth.
- **Read and reflect on scripture passages** about aging and the promise of eternal life. Psalms, the wisdom books, and other biblical texts are powerful tools that offer comfort and insight.
- **Recite the Official Prayer of the Church,** "Liturgy of the Hours." If you can go to Church, participate in Mass. It will also provide you with an opportunity to connect with people.
- **Reflect on life's meaning:** Contemplating the meaning of life will help you prioritize your priorities more meaningfully every day. You could take meditative walks or discuss your priorities with trusted friends or spiritual advisors.
- **Reflect on your life story** as it fits into God's larger plan for creation and redemption. This could be done in sharing sessions, too.

Make sure to do these regularly.
Set apart a time for each.

. . .

Community and Fellowship

- **Participate in your Church's activities,** such as fellowship gatherings, celebrations, or small group study sessions, that give you the opportunity to share your wisdom and knowledge. Your spiritual journey with others will deepen your sense of belonging.
- **Participate in special fund-raising programs** for the Church or community is an excellent way to show that you care, even if it is in a small way. Don't always be a consumer; be a graceful giver as well. Remember what St. Paul told the Corinthians, "Each one giving, just as he has determined in his heart, neither out of sadness nor out of obligation. For God loves a cheerful giver." (2 Cor. 9: 7)
- **Get a church bulletin or email communication** of the parish and keep up with what is happening. Utilize the opportunities for communal prayer, study, and enrichment programs that nurture your spiritual life and provide companionship.

Foster Spiritual Resilience

- **Embrace the changes:** Accept the physical and psychological changes accompanying aging as part of God's plan. Our bodily and mental faculties fade as a prelude to the soul leaving our body. Hearing less, seeing less, grasping, and comprehending less are the ways we gradually withdraw from this world. (We probably don't want to hear or see everything happening around us for better peace of mind.)
- **Practice forgiveness**, both towards others and to yourself. Letting go of the past hurts liberates us to live

more fully in the present and to enjoy calmness and peace of mind. So, let go.

Cultivate Mindfulness

Mindfulness can reduce stress, enhance emotional well-being, and keep you calm, no matter what. It will also help you appreciate the beauty and significance of everyday experiences.

Therefore,

- **"Take time to 'Smell the Roses.'** This reminds us to slow down and appreciate the beauty around us. Surround yourself with beauty, whether in nature, art, music, or relationships. Embrace activities that bring you joy and refresh your spirit.
- **Engage in creative activities** that express your talents and skills. This could be anything from painting or writing to volunteering in your community. These activities meaningfully express your inner self and might result in a valuable contribution to society.

In Summary

Never think of aging as a process of physical decline but a time of immense spiritual potential. By acknowledging and fostering the gifts of wisdom, gratitude, and spiritual growth, we can transform our twilight years into a meaningful period of enrichment and fulfillment. Embracing the spirituality of aging helps us to deepen our relationship with God and approach the end of life with grace and hope. Through intentional practices to build a resilient spirit and connection with God, we can transform the aging process into one of dignity, joy, and purposefulness.

Chapter 33
The Eucharist And Aging
Nourishing The Soul For The Journey

Aging brings a profound opportunity for deeper reflection on life's journey. As physical strength wanes and the distractions of earlier years fade, the Eucharist becomes the central act of worship and a source of spiritual sustenance, healing, and renewal. In the later years of life, the Eucharist is no longer just a ritual but a genuine encounter with Christ that offers comfort, strength, and a foretaste of eternal communion with God.

This chapter explores the profound relationship between the **Eucharist and aging,** its theological significance for those in later life, and how it serves as both a spiritual anchor and an invitation to a more profound union with Christ.

1. The Eucharist as Sustenance for the Journey

Throughout life, we partake in the Eucharist as a sacred act of worship, but as we age, it takes on an even deeper significance. It is no longer simply a habit or tradition—it becomes a spiritual necessity. For those who have faced loss, illness, or physical decline, the

Eucharist offers strength for the present moment and hope for the future.

- **Manna in the Desert:** Just as God provided manna for the Israelites in the wilderness **(Exodus 16:4)**, the Eucharist is our sustenance as we walk through the desert of aging. This bread strengthens us when we feel weak and sustains us when we feel uncertain.
- **Daily Bread for Spiritual Strength**: Jesus teaches us to pray, "Give us this day our daily bread" **(Matthew 6:11)**. For aging individuals, the Eucharist becomes this daily bread—not just physically received but spiritually internalized, nourishing the soul as we journey toward eternity.

2. Healing and Wholeness: The Eucharist as Medicine for the Soul

Aging often brings physical suffering, emotional loneliness, and spiritual dryness. Many struggle with chronic illness, grief over lost loved ones, or a sense of diminished purpose. The Eucharist becomes a healing balm in these struggles, offering divine comfort and renewal.

- **The Eucharist and the Healing Ministry of Christ:** Jesus healed the sick and restored the brokenhearted. He continues to heal us through the Eucharist. It is not only a meal but medicine for the soul.

- **Inner Healing Through Communion:** St. Augustine called the Eucharist "the medicine of immortality" because it strengthens us from within. Receiving Christ in the Eucharist allows us to surrender our pains, fears, and weaknesses to Him.

- **Healing Beyond the Physical:** While the Eucharist does not remove physical suffering, it offers spiritual healing—a deep sense of peace, renewal, and reassurance that we are not alone in our trials.

3. A Foretaste of Heaven

The Eucharist bridges the present and eternity for those in the later seasons of life. It reminds us that our earthly journey is not the final destination but a passage toward something greater.

- **A Preview of the Heavenly Banquet:** The Eucharist is a foretaste of the **wedding feast of the Lamb (Revelation 19:9)**, where all believers will be united with Christ in eternal joy. Each time we receive Communion, we are reminded that this life is a preparation for something far more glorious.

- **Union with the Saints and Departed Loved Ones**: In the Eucharistic celebration, we are mystically united with the entire Body of Christ—those on earth, those in purgatory, and those in heaven. This is the best source of comfort for the elderly, who may have lost spouses, siblings, or lifelong friends.

- **Anticipating the Final Journey**: Our perspective on life shifts as we age. The Eucharist reassures us that death is not an end but a passage into a deeper union with Christ. It transforms fear into trust, anxiety into peace, and uncertainty into hope.

4. Challenges of Access for the Elderly

While the Eucharist remains central to the spiritual life of aging individuals, many seniors face challenges in regularly attending Mass. Some are homebound, others live in assisted care facilities, and some struggle with transportation.

- **The Need for Eucharistic Ministers to the Homebound:** Parishes recognize the importance of bringing the Eucharist to those who cannot attend Mass. This is not merely a pastoral duty but a continuation of Christ's mission to seek out and care for His flock.

- **Spiritual Communion for the Homebound**: Even when physically receiving the Eucharist is not possible, seniors can make an act of spiritual communion, inviting Christ into their hearts and uniting themselves spiritually to the Eucharistic celebration.

- **Creative Parish Outreach:** Communities should explore ways to include the elderly in Eucharistic celebrations, whether through live-streamed Masses, visits from clergy, or designated transportation services.

5. The Eucharist and the Call to Let Go

As we grow older, the Eucharist teaches us the grace of surrender. It reminds us that just as Christ gave Himself entirely in the Eucharist, we too are called to let go—of our attachments, fears, and even our lives—and surrender them into God's hands, as discussed in the previous chapter.

- **Letting Go of Control:** Aging often means surrendering independence, but the Eucharist teaches us that surrender is not weakness—but trust. Just as Jesus surrendered Himself in love on the cross, we must also learn to trust in God's perfect timing and providence.

- **Letting Go of Past Regrets:** The Eucharist is a sacrament of reconciliation as well. It reminds us that God's mercy is more significant than our mistakes and that our past does not define us.

- **Letting Go into Eternal Life**: Finally, the Eucharist prepares us for the ultimate surrender—entrusting our souls completely to God at the moment of death. Each Mass becomes a rehearsal for our final "Amen" to the Lord.

6. Living the Eucharistic Life in Old Age

The Eucharist is not just something we receive; we are called to live out. Even with the limitations of aging, seniors can embody the Eucharist in their daily lives.

- **Becoming Bread for Others:** Just as Jesus gives Himself in the Eucharist, seniors can offer themselves in love—through words of wisdom, acts of kindness, and being a source of encouragement.

- **Offering Suffering as a Eucharistic Sacrifice**: Those who endure illness or suffering can unite their pain with Christ's sacrifice, transforming it into a powerful prayer for others.

- **Fostering Gratitude and Joy:** As the Eucharist means "thanksgiving," seniors can model gratitude by living each day with a spirit of thanksgiving for God's blessings.

Conclusion: The Eucharist—A Journey Home

For the aging soul, the Eucharist is the compass that points toward home. It is both nourishment for the present and a promise of what will come. It unites the soul with Christ.

As we partake in the Eucharist, we are reminded that we are never alone, and that when the final moment comes, we will be stepping into the radiant light of eternal communion with God.

Chapter 34
Gifts and Blessings of Aging

Aging is very often viewed as a process of decline and loss. However, people with a vision rooted in the Christian faith see it as a reservoir of profound gifts and blessings. As we embrace the later stages of life, we discover that aging is not a burden but a sacred pilgrimage of the soul — a journey that invites us to discover and cultivate the unique virtues that come with age — wisdom, gratitude, and spiritual growth.

Let us consider some of the blessings of age and how we can fruitfully utilize them.

"Be Wise" (Matthew 10:16)

Perhaps wisdom is the most cherished gift we get with aging. Wisdom transcends mere knowledge. It is fashioned in the crucible of experience, tempered by the passage of time, and refined through life's joys and sorrows, triumphs and tribulations. Amidst life's trials and tribulations, we can garner insights, deepen our understanding of human frailty and limitations, and be practical about the need to build resilience.

Every challenge of our life has contributed toward the refinement of our wisdom. Unlike knowledge, wisdom encompasses a deep understanding of life's complexities and nuances. It helps us see beyond immediate concerns and comprehend the broader meaning and relevance of existence.

Like the wine aging in oak barrels, wisdom is tempered by the passage of time. Through the ebbs and flows of time, we receive a mature perspective that allows us to see beyond the immediacy of each moment. Moreover, we get the quality of a unique perception to discern the patterns and rhythms of the threads of experience intertwined through the fabric of our existence. It helps us to embrace the beauty of life's grace and gifts while perceiving its transiency.

With their wealth of experience and good judgment, seniors often possess insights and a broader perspective that can guide and inspire younger generations. It is essential to pause and reflect on the profound depth of our wisdom so that we can use it to profit others.

"Be Thankful" (1 Thessalonians 5:18)

The fabulous aging phenomenon makes us see the fleeting nature of life's moments. As we age, we become increasingly aware of the abundance of blessings surrounding us in every moment. This awareness fosters a deep sense of gratitude in us. We recognize that despite life's challenges and uncertainties, there is always something to be grateful for.

This awareness should fill our hearts with a deep sense of gratitude. We appreciate even the simple joys and the beauty of everyday experiences. It helps to foster the transformative power of gratitude that enhances not only our well-being but also radiates its positivity around us. Gratitude, in reality, shifts our focus from what we lack to what we have, cultivating a spirit of thankfulness for the blessings, big or small, that we have received. Thus, gratitude grants us a spirit of joy, resilience, and contentment, embracing each day as a precious gift from God.

Resilience (James 1:2-4)

Life in later years often brings its share of challenges: the aches of a body that has known many seasons, the quiet loneliness that sometimes accompanies change, and the inevitable reflections on loss and memories. Yet, it is precisely through these trials that resilience is forged. It is the gentle art of bouncing back and acknowledging our struggles while embracing the strength within us.

A powerful way to build this resilience is through **the practice of mindfulness.** Imagine sitting quietly in a familiar, comfortable space, focusing on the rhythm of your breath and feeling the pulse of life in each moment. Being present and grounding yourself in the here and now offers a sanctuary from the turbulence of worry and regret. It allows you to savor the present moment's sweetness, find peace in the stillness, and gradually cultivate an inner reserve of calm.

In Conclusion

We discover that life is not measured by the passing of years but by the richness of our experiences and the expansiveness of our hearts. It helps us acknowledge with gratitude all our blessings from God and appreciate the depth of relationships we build in life.

Therefore, the journey through the later stages of our life should be imbued with the desire to embrace each day with open hearts, trusting in the unfolding of life's divine purpose. As we open our hearts to the abundance of blessings surrounding us, our thoughts should rise up to the one who has granted all these. Hence, our exploration of the gift of aging should lead to deepening our connection to the divine that infuses every moment of our life with meaning, purpose, and life itself.

Tailpiece

At the reunion of a graduating class of girls, they agreed to meet every ten years at a restaurant to recollect their old memories. At age 50, they decided to go to the 'Little Garden Grill' because the servers there were cute young men. At age 60, they decided to go to 'Little Garden Grill' because the food there was excellent. At age 70, they decided to go to the 'Little Garden Grill' restaurant because it had handicapped access. At age 80, they decided to go to 'Little Garden Grill' because they had never gone there.

Chapter 35
Grandparenting as a Spiritual Vocation

Aging is not just about personal growth; but also about leaving a legacy. Among the greatest blessings of later life is the opportunity to be a grandparent—not just biologically but spiritually as well.

Grandparenting is a sacred vocation, a calling to pass down wisdom, values, and faith to younger generations. This chapter explores the biblical foundation of grandparenting, its importance in faith formation, and the practical ways grandparents can nurture spirituality within their families.

1. The Unique Role of Grandparents in Faith Formation

- Grandparents serve as storytellers, mentors, and spiritual guides within their families.
- Unlike parents, whose role is often tied to discipline and daily responsibilities, grandparents offer a gentler, more reflective presence in a child's life.

- Research shows that children with strong relationships with their grandparents are more likely to hold onto religious beliefs into adulthood.
- The wisdom of experience gives grandparents a different perspective that can reassure and inspire younger generations.

The Grandparent-Grandchild Bond: A Source of Spiritual Stability

- Many children listen differently to their grandparents than to their parents.
- Grandparents can become a safe place where grandchildren feel loved and understood.
- **Grandparents can be a child's primary spiritual influence i**n broken or non-religious families.

2. Biblical and Theological Perspectives on Passing Down Faith

The Scriptures place great emphasis on generational faith transmission. The wisdom of elders was not just respected but considered essential for the continuity of God's covenant.

- **Deuteronomy 4:9** – "You should not forget the things that your eyes have seen and do not let them be cut away from your heart, throughout all the days of your life. You shall teach them to your sons and to your grandsons."
- **Psalm 145:4** – "Generation after generation will praise your works, and they will declare your power."
- **2 Timothy 1:5** – Paul reminds Timothy of the faith he

inherited from his grandmother, Lois, and his mother, Eunice.

In many cultures, elders passed down skills and moral and religious teachings. Grandparents today continue that role by sharing stories of faith, praying with their families, and modeling Christian virtues in their daily lives.

Spiritual Grandparenting Beyond Blood Relatives

- Not everyone has grandchildren, but spiritual grandparenting **e**xtends beyond biological ties.
- Seniors in churches and communities can mentor younger generations, offering wisdom and guidance as spiritual elders.
- Older adults can serve as adoptive grandparents to children in their parishes, neighborhoods, or ministries.

3. Practical Ways to Nurture Family Spirituality

Faith formation is more than teaching—it is about living faith in a way that makes it real and relevant to younger generations.

a. Sharing Faith Stories

- Grandparents hold **family history** and spiritual experiences that younger generations may never know unless shared.
- **Telling stories of God's faithfulness**—whether through personal struggles, answered prayers, or family traditions—can inspire and strengthen faith in younger hearts.
- **Keep a spiritual journal** or write letters to grandchildren, sharing faith lessons.

b. Praying with and for Grandchildren

- Establishing prayer traditions, such as:
  - **Praying before meals and bedtime** when visiting.
  - **Encouraging grandchildren to call for prayer requests.**
  - **Praying a blessing over them** before they leave after a visit.
- Let grandchildren see faith in action through daily devotions, reading Scripture, and **attending church together.**

c. Passing Down Family and Religious Traditions

- Observing holidays with faith-based customs, such as Advent candle lighting or reading the Nativity story at Christmas.
- Teaching grandchildren hymns, Bible verses, and prayers that were meaningful in your own childhood.
- Sharing cultural or ethnic traditions that have spiritual significance.

d. Being Present in Their Lives

- **Making intentional time** for visits, phone calls, or video chats.
- **Attending their important events**, such as baptisms, confirmations, or even school plays.
- **Sending handwritten notes** of encouragement, especially when they are struggling.

e. Modeling Faith Through Actions

- **Living out** kindness, patience, forgiveness, and generosity.
- **Demonstrating** how to trust God in difficult times.
- **Volunteering** or serving in the church together to encourage a spirit of giving.

4. Overcoming Challenges in Grandparenting

Not all families are religious, and not all grandchildren are receptive to faith discussions.

a. Navigating Faith Differences

- Some grandparents find themselves in secular families where faith is not actively practiced.
- Instead of forcing faith, live it authentically—letting love and example speak louder than words.
- Ask, **"How can I show them Christ through my actions?"** rather than, "How can I convince them?"
- **Never compromise your faith convictions** to please them or "not to offend them," as some people would say.

b. When Grandchildren are Distant

- In cases where physical distance prevents regular visits, technology can bridge the gap.
- Use video calls, letters, emails, or recorded prayers to stay connected.
- Send faith-based books, devotionals, or handwritten Bible verses to encourage spiritual reflection.

5. The Blessing of Grandparenting

Grand-parenting is more than a biological role—it is a sacred calling. It offers a final, beautiful opportunity to shape future generations in faith. Whether by sharing stories, praying together, or simply living as a witness to God's love, grandparents have a unique and irreplaceable role in the spiritual lives of their families.

Rather than seeing aging as a loss of purpose, it is an invitation to a new kind of vocation—one of guidance, mentorship, and legacy-building.

We leave behind not just possessions but faith, wisdom, and a testimony of God's faithfulness that can echo for generations.

Reflection Questions: How has a grandparent or elder influenced your faith journey?How can you be more intentional about sharing your faith with younger generations?

- How can you continue your spiritual vocation, even if your family is not religious?

Chapter 36
Surrounded by Family

Elizabeth and her husband Robert, were longtime members of the parish. Their kindness and dedication were evident in every act of service. They both served as Extraordinary Ministers of the Eucharist and organized Communion services at the nearby nursing home. Their warm smiles and Elizabeth's gentle, loving voice endeared them to everyone.

Their presence was woven into the heart of the parish, and their generosity was evident not just in what they did but also in who they were.

A Life of Service and Love

Every First Friday, Elizabeth and Robert used to organize Communion Service for the nursing home residents and invited the pastor to lead it. Elizabeth promptly arranged separate rooms for Confession and Communion Service.

The residents, eager for spiritual nourishment, would already be waiting. After the Penance Service, Confession, and Communion,

Elizabeth and Robert would walk the pastor down to his car. Their kindness never failed to touch his heart.

That was who they were—always serving, always giving, always making sure others were cared for.

A Sudden Decline

Over the years, the pastor watched them grow older, their strength gradually fading. Yet, Elizabeth's spirit remained undimmed.

Then, one morning, a call from the hospital came:

"Father, Elizabeth is in the ICU. Robert is requesting Anointing of the Sick and Communion for her."

The pastor was shocked—what had happened so suddenly?

Robert stood outside her room when he arrived, looking weary but composed. He explained that Elizabeth had been battling severe bronchial issues due to inherited asthma. Over time, her condition worsened, and even the portable oxygen tank she always carried was no longer sufficient. The doctors were not optimistic about her recovery.

When the pastor entered the room, Elizabeth greeted him with her characteristic enthusiasm despite her frail state. She smiled as though nothing had changed.

The pastor prepared to give her the Anointing of the Sick. But she had another plan: "Father, would you be kind enough to come tomorrow? I have asked all my children and grandchildren to be here tomorrow. I want to receive the Last Sacrament in their presence and say goodbye to everyone." He stood there, marveling at her strength, faith, and unwavering peace.

As he stepped outside, Robert's voice was tinged with sorrow and resignation:

"The doctor says she is in critical condition, and she will have to be moved to hospice care tomorrow."

Final Goodbyes

The next day, Elizabeth was transferred to hospice care. She gathered her children and grandchildren, saying her goodbyes to each of them.

"Father, Elizabeth thinks it may be her time to go. She wants to see you and the Sisters of our parish. She wants to say her final goodbyes."

The news left the pastor momentarily speechless. He assured him he would go there as soon as possible.

When they arrived, Elizabeth, though visibly weakened, greeted them with the same warm smile. She hugged them tightly, holding their hands as she spoke, her voice now strained but still filled with love.

Together, they recited Psalm 23:

"The Lord is my Shepherd, I shall not want... Even though I walk through the valley of the shadow of death, I will fear no evil, for You are with me."

The pastor gave her the final blessing, and everyone stood in profound silence, the weight of farewell heavy in their minds.

As they turned to leave, they saw her still smiling, full of grace, a beacon of peace and acceptance. Two days later, she passed away peacefully, surrounded by love, family, and faith.

Everyone knew that when she met her Creator, it was with the same radiant smile that had touched so many lives.

Elizabeth's life was not just one of service—but of love, lived fully until the very end.

Chapter 37
Family and Community Connections

Relationships have a deep connection with happiness and contentment in the journey of aging. As we traverse the terrain of later life, we discover that our connections with others, whether family, friends, or faith communities, provide essential support, companionship, and purposefulness.

A network of relationships can sustain us through life's joys and struggles. Our interaction with others, especially those who share our journey, offers us solace, solidarity, and a sense of belonging. It nurtures our well-being and enriches our lives with shared experiences and a sense of belonging.

Family Connections

Family is the primary support system for older adults. The bonds of kindred provide emotional sustenance, happiness, and a sense of belonging. It is a fact that children and grandchildren of elderly people are always busy. Nonetheless, it is essential that they intentionally contact and visit their elderly parents or grandparents, especially on special occasions such as their birthdays and celebrations such as Thanksgiving, Christmas, Easter, etc.

Invite them to your family gatherings or bring them if they cannot travel alone. Young parents should teach their children about the need to connect with older adults in the family. These are some of the ways you make them feel valued. Moreover, such family gatherings can strengthen bonds and provide opportunities for connection and support. In many families, it is a tradition to have the presence of the elderly at family celebrations.

In such gatherings, make sure that children engage in open communication with them. Engage them in shared activities everyone enjoys, such as cooking meals, playing games, and other family traditions and hobbies. Plan activities that integrate all family members, from the youngest to the oldest, creating opportunities for bonding and mutual support. The young ones will learn many lessons and hear exciting stories of life experiences from older people. And encourage open communication about their needs, expectations, and plans for the future. Ensure that everyone, especially children, is a part of such sharing. It should also be a "cell phone-down" day.

Friends

Friendships provide unique companionship and support, especially with people with shared experiences and interests. Church groups, golf buddies, people of the same profession, and neighborhood companions can enrich each other through their get-togethers. Participate in outings, restaurant gatherings, hobby groups, etc. It is advisable to establish support networks where friends can rely on each other for help with daily tasks or even companionship during rough times. Therefore, stay connected through phone calls, video chats, or meet-ups.

Faith Communities

Church-related groups can provide more than just companionship. They can offer spiritual nourishment, social interaction, and a great sense of belonging. Participation in worship services offers both spiritual fulfillment and community connection with purpose. Join small groups for Bible study, prayer, and discussions that help create a more intimate sense of community and belonging. Volunteer opportunities at Church or other community centers foster a sense of purpose and service.

The Next Chapter is a real story that shows how meaningful family connections are.

Chapter 38
Relationships Matter

John and Mary Walters, once the heart and soul of our parish, now face a quiet yet heartbreaking struggle.

In their golden years, they were everywhere—John, the cornerstone of the Men's Club, organizing events with infectious enthusiasm, and Mary, always by his side, volunteering and extending a helping hand wherever needed. They lived for their parish community, filling it with love, laughter, and tireless service.

But as time wore on, maintaining their cherished home became too much. With reluctance and heavy hearts, they sold it and moved into a nursing home, hoping for comfort and companionship but finding loneliness instead.

The bustling life they once knew faded away, replaced by the monotony of their new surroundings. Friends from the parish gradually lost touch, their absence a silent reminder of the harsh reality that too often, "out of sight, out of mind" prevails.

A Hidden Struggle

When I visited the nursing home, I found John and Mary rarely left their room. The caretaker, with a hint of sorrow, revealed their hidden struggle—they had retreated into themselves, finding solace in alcohol.

Their once vibrant presence had dimmed, and their room was no longer filled with joy and laughter but with the stench of stale food and despair.

A Painful Truth

Determined to help, I reached out to their son. After some gentle prodding, he shared a painful truth:

- After selling their home, John and Mary donated much of their money to cancer research in memory of the daughter they had lost to cancer.
- They also gave generously to another daughter who seldom showed them love. For some reason, the son felt that he got very little.
- Feeling abandoned and betrayed, their son distanced himself, leaving his parents even more isolated.

A Call to Remember Those Who Once Cared for Us

John and Mary, who had given the community so much love, energy, and life, were now forgotten, enveloped in loneliness and sorrow.

Their story is a poignant reminder of our duty to care for those who once cared for us.

Let us not let their light fade away unnoticed.

Chapter 39
Nurturing Joy and Peace in Later Life

Aging gracefully means more than merely passing time —it is about rediscovering a reservoir of joy and vitality hidden in the simplicity of each day. This chapter explores five transformative practices that encourage us to embrace life with a renewed sense of purpose and delight.

As we journey through the later chapters of life, we often discover that joy does not simply vanish with the passing of our youth —it transforms, deepens, and becomes intricately woven into the fabric of our everyday existence. Imagine waking up to a soft, golden light streaming through your window, the gentle rustling of leaves in the morning breeze, and the promise that each new day holds an opportunity for wonder. This is the beginning of nurturing joy in our later years—a practice of finding beauty in the ordinary and the extraordinary alike.

In these moments, joy is not a fleeting emotion but a steady, grounding force. It is the smile shared over a cup of tea with an old friend, the laughter that bubbles up during a heartfelt conversation, or the silent gratitude that fills your soul as you watch the sunset. It is about reconnecting with the simple pleasures that once made our hearts sing **a**nd allowing those moments to guide us toward a more profound sense of fulfillment.

1. Wonder of Everyday Moments

In the rush of our earlier busy years, we often overlooked the beauty of the ordinary. Now, as the pace of life gently slows, there is an invitation to rediscover the simple pleasures that make each day unique. Imagine the warmth of sunlight on your face during a morning walk, the soothing aroma of a home-cooked meal, or the serene pleasure of a quiet moment with a good book. You reclaim a sense of wonder and fulfillment by intentionally savoring these moments. In embracing these small joys, you create a more mindful existence and build a foundation of contentment that brightens even the most challenging days.

2. The Power of Gratitude

Gratitude is a transformative force that reshapes our perception of the world. Focusing on what we have rather than what we lack unlocks a deep reservoir of emotional strength. Consider keeping **a** daily gratitude journal—each entry a testament to life's blessings, from the laughter of a loved one to the simple gift of a beautiful day. This practice nurtures a positive mindset and connects you to a higher sense of purpose. In every moment of thankfulness, you reinforce the idea that every breath and encounter is a cherished part of your life's tapestry.

3. New Hobbies and Interests

There is a thrill in the discovery that remains timeless. Whether learning a new instrument, dabbling in painting, gardening, or even taking up a new sport, exploring new hobbies awakens dormant passions and ignites curiosity.

For example, I have always wanted to write fiction and non-fiction books, but this has never happened during my rather busy pastoral life. After retirement, I decided to follow my passion for writing. In a year and a half, I finished three books—this being the second—and two more are on the way. When people ask me how my retirement life is, my answer is, "I enjoy it very much." Now, I feel that 24 hours a day is never enough—but in a nice way.

These pursuits invite you to step out of familiar patterns and open yourself up to fresh experiences and communities. By challenging yourself to learn something new and start something you have always wanted to do, you not only enhance your cognitive vitality but also infuse your days with excitement and purpose. Each new interest is an opportunity to rewrite the narrative of aging as a dynamic journey filled with endless possibilities.

4. Laughter the Best Medicine

Laughter is a universal language that binds us together, and its benefits extend far beyond the momentary spark of joy. Embracing humor in everyday life allows you to view challenges through a lighter lens, softening the edges of stress and worry. Recall a time when a shared joke or a playful moment brought warmth to your heart—humor has the remarkable power to heal and unite.

Whether it's enjoying a comedy show, sharing humorous memories with friends, or simply learning to laugh at life's little quirks, nurturing a sense of humor enriches your emotional well-being and reminds you that joy is always within reach. During my travels, I've observed many seniors gathering at their favorite rural restaurants for brunch, spending hours in lively conversation and hearty laughter. So, get out and connect with others—it's an excellent way to keep your spirits high.

5. Finding Serenity in the Divine

A deep spiritual connection is at the core of lasting happiness—a source of joy and peace that transcends the physical world. Whether you find solace in prayer, meditation, or quiet reflection in nature, embracing your spiritual side offers a sanctuary of calm amid life's turbulence. This inward journey connects you with a higher purpose and infuses each day with meaning. You invite serenity, hope, and an abiding sense of inner light by cultivating practices that nurture your spirit. In a sacred space, you discover that true joy is not a fleeting emotion but a continuous presence that enriches every aspect of your life.

Nurturing these practices—**cherishing simple pleasures, practicing gratitude, exploring new interests, embracing humor, and seeking spiritual peace**—empowers you to live each day with intention and delight. After all, in later years, life can be a celebration of both the wisdom we have gathered and the beauty that still awaits discovery.

This chapter gently reminds us that aging is not a decline but an evolving journey, rich with opportunities to grow, connect, and find joy in every moment.

Chapter 40
The Grace Of Letting Go
Detachment And Spiritual Freedom

Aging often brings with it a profound reckoning with what truly matters. Over the years, people accumulate not just material possessions but also expectations, attachments, regrets, and fears.

Yet, as physical strength diminishes, God invites us to a deeper journey of detachment, surrender, and true spiritual freedom. This chapter explores the grace of letting go and how aging can be a time of liberation rather than loss.

1. The Invitation to Detachment: Aging as a Spiritual Awakening

- **Aging naturally forces detachment:** children grow up and become independent, careers come to an end, and the body slows down.
- Rather than viewing these changes as losses, they can be embraced as opportunities for spiritual deepening.
- The call of Christ to **"leave all things and follow Him"** takes on new meaning in later years.

. . .

2. The Weight of Material Attachments

- Many people find it difficult to relinquish their material possessions, clinging to them as symbols of identity and security.
- Downsizing, giving away treasured items, or selling a home can feel like losing a part of oneself.
- Simplifying life can be a spiritual practice, freeing the soul from excess burdens.

3. Letting Go of Expectations and Regrets

- The later years often bring reflections on what could have been—dreams unfulfilled, mistakes made, relationships lost. Avoid saying, "I could have" and "I should have."
- **Carrying regret weighs down the heart** and prevents spiritual freedom.
- True detachment means accepting God's providence in all things and trusting that everything in life—both joys and sorrows—has served a purpose.

4. Lessons from Christian Mysticism: St. John of the Cross and St. Teresa of Ávila

- **St. John of the Cross**'s "Dark Night of the Soul": How trials and suffering purify the heart, leading to a deeper union with God.

- **St. Teresa**'s "Interior Castle": Moving away from superficial attachments into the deeper rooms of the soul where God dwells.
- **What These Teachings Mean** for Aging: Viewing the aging process as a natural movement toward divine intimacy rather than something to be feared.

5. Finding Joy in Simplicity and Trust in God's Providence

- **Living with gratitude for each moment** rather than longing for what has passed.
- Finding peace in knowing that God is enough—that spiritual strength can grow even as physical strength fades.
- Use **the Serenity Prayer** as a Model for Aging Well: "God, grant me the serenity to accept the things I cannot change, courage to change the things I can, and wisdom to know the difference."[1]

Conclusion

In a world that often fears old age and clings to worldly attachments, these thoughts offer an invitation to something more significant: **the joy of surrender, the peace of trust, and the ultimate freedom found in faith**.

---

1. The Serenity Prayer - Reinhold Niebuhr, a Lutheran theologian (1892–1971)

Chapter 41
Cultivating a Sense of Legacy

The concept of legacy is at the heart of the search for meaning and purpose in later life. It's the mark we leave on the world and future generations. We can see how our lives intersect with others, shaping the history of our community and our Church in various ways. Through acts of kindness, compassion, and generosity, we can plant seeds of hope and inspiration that endure long after we're gone, leaving a lasting legacy of love.

Extending this legacy beyond our family's boundaries can often be more meaningful and fulfilling. In many dioceses, **Catholic Foundations** provide opportunities and inspiration to create lasting legacies in diverse ways. This emphasis on legacy underscores our value and significance, making us feel genuinely appreciated and essential.

Thus, we will discover that the true essence of our humanity lies not just in the accumulation of wealth, power, influence, or prestige but instead in the relationships we forge in life, the values we embody, the kindness and generosity we show, and the legacy we leave behind.

Practical Tips to Prepare for the Inevitable Moment

1. **Engaging in contemplative practices** such as prayer, meditation, reflection on sacred texts, and reading the lives of saints deepen our understanding of death and the afterlife. It will bring about a sense of peace and acceptance.

2. **Do practical preparations,** such as creating advance directives (legal documents that specify your healthcare preferences if you become unable to make decisions) and discussing end-of-life wishes with loved ones. Planning funeral rites, including the type of service and any specific requests you may have, can also provide clarity and reduce anxiety about what is to come. Consider how you wish to be remembered and what legacy you want to leave behind.

3. **Engage in meaningful activities** that share your wisdom and knowledge, such as mentoring younger community members, volunteering for charitable causes, or leading spiritual discussions. These activities can help you feel connected and valued and ensure that your life continues to have an impact after you are gone.

4. **Keep up meaningful relationships** to ensure that your life continues to have an impact after you are gone.

5. **Seek support from your Church community,** your pastors, or spiritual leaders, and, if necessary, from counseling services. It can provide you comfort and guidance as you navigate the spiritual dimensions of death.

In Conclusion

Finding meaning and purpose in later life is a journey that involves more than just aging gracefully and spiritually. It's about embracing the spiritual and biblical foundations of purpose, exploring new avenues of fulfillment, and engaging in community. But it's also about fostering healthy relationships, a source of resilience and joy.

By being earnestly involved in activities for charitable causes, we can navigate this journey with a deep sense of purpose, a steadfast commitment to love, and a profound reverence for the sacredness of every moment. This will help us approach the end of life with grace, hope, and a deep sense of communion with the divine.

Chapter 42
Habits To Build
And Habits To Watch For

Habits are the invisible architects of identity. They are consistent, often unconscious actions woven into one's life and they shape one's character, attitudes, and behaviour.

1 Habits Matter in Aging

- Our habits shape our physical, emotional, and spiritual well-being, and they become even more important in later years.
- Unlike the sudden changes of youth, aging is often a gradual transformation, and our daily routines determine our quality of life.
- We now explore which habits enrich aging and which may lead to decline—not just physically but also mentally and spiritually.

2 Habits for a Fulfilling Old Age

a. Cultivating a Daily Prayer and Reflection Routine

- Aging offers more time for contemplation and deeper prayer.
- Establish a consistent time for prayer (morning, evening, before meals) nurtures the soul.
- Be aware of the role of Scripture, the Rosary, and journaling in spiritual enrichment.

b. Prioritizing Physical Movement

- Exercise doesn't have to be intense—regular walking, stretching, and deep breathing improves longevity.
- Proper nutrition, hydration, and good sleep hygiene support a healthy body and mind.
- Regular medical check-ups help with the early detection of age-related issues.

c. Maintaining Social Connections

- **Loneliness** is one of the greatest risks for seniors—prioritizing relationships keeps the mind and heart active.
- **Staying connected** with family, friends, parish communities, and senior groups provides a sense of belonging.
- **Intergenerational friendships** offer a fresh perspective and strengthen bonds with younger generations.

d. Practicing Gratitude and Letting Go of Regrets

- Developing a habit of daily gratitude counters negative thinking and increases joy.
- Letting go of past hurts and regrets leads to spiritual and emotional freedom.
- The Eucharist is a reminder of God's providence and a call to thank Him.

e. Keeping the Mind Active Through Learning and Creativity

- Engage in **lifelong learning**—reading, writing, taking courses, or picking up new hobbies.
- **Art, music, gardening, or storytelling** keeps the mind sharp.
- **Avoid mental stagnation** by challenging the brain with puzzles, discussions, and new skills.

3. Habits to Watch For and Avoid
a. Isolation and Withdrawal

- **Shutting oneself away** from social circles may lead to loneliness and depression.
- Excuses like "I don't want to be a burden" often lead to **self-imposed isolation**.
- See the importance of **active engagement** in community and faith life.

b. Excessive Worry and Fear

- **Anxiety about health, finances, or the future** can lead to constant stress.
- Trusting in God's plan and **developing a habit of surrender** eases worry.

- Turn to **prayer, Scripture, and positive affirmations** instead of falling into fear-based thinking.

c. Neglecting Physical Health

- Ignoring proper nutrition, hydration, and movement can lead to deterioration of health.
- **"I'm too old to exercise" is a myth**—small movements help preserve independence.
- **Avoiding medical check-ups** due to fear of bad news is counterproductive.

d. Holding Onto Bitterness and Unforgiveness

- Carrying **resentment** is emotionally and spiritually damaging.
- Learning to release grudges through forgiveness brings peace in later years.
- Reconciliation with family, old friends, and even oneself can be deeply healing.

Sacrament of Reconciliation is an excellent spiritual antidote for guilt feelings.

e. Becoming Spiritually Passive

- Some seniors stop actively participating in their faith, thinking, "**I've done enough.**"
- But **spiritual growth never stops**—new insights continue unfolding until our final breath.
- **Find renewed purpose** in mentorship, prayer, and parish involvement.

4. The Theology of Forming Holy Habits in Old Age

- Scripture reminds us that we are called to continual renewal:
  - **Romans 12:2** – "Do not choose to be conformed to this age, but instead choose to be reformed in the newness of your mind."
  - **Psalm 92:14** – "They will still bear fruit in old age, and they will endure well."
- **Saints like St. Benedict and St. Ignatius of Loyola** emphasized the **power** of daily habits in shaping a holy life.
- The aging years are not a time of decline but a sacred period of refinement—a preparation for eternal life.

5. Practical Steps for Building Holy Habits

- **Start small and consistent**—it's about daily efforts, not grand gestures.
- Find an **accountability partner** (a spouse, friend, or fellow churchgoer) to encourage growth.
- Keep a **"Rule of Life"**—a structured daily plan for prayer, physical well-being, relationships, and lifelong learning.

Conclusion: The Path to Holistic and Holy Aging

- Our **daily habits** determine the quality of our later years—spiritually, emotionally, and physically.
- By **embracing good habits** and avoiding destructive ones, seniors can experience peace, joy, and fulfillment.
- Aging with purpose means **trusting in God,** nurturing relationships, and continually growing in faith.

- **Practical and Theological**: It integrates spiritual wisdom with real-life application.

- **Encourages Active Participation**: Many seniors struggle with the fear of losing purpose—this chapter helps them reclaim it.
- **Addresses Common Challenges**: Tackle loneliness, negativity, and health concerns while offering faith-based solutions.

Chapter 43
Appearance And Self-Care

Do we need to care about our appearance? Does it really matter?

Not many people realize that self-care in old age is highly relevant to mental health, as it often reflects a person's inner state—both positively and negatively. It adds a valuable dimension to our discussion of habits that nurture or harm well-being.

The Connection Between Appearance and Mental Well-being

As we age, how we care for ourselves externally mirrors what's happening internally—in our emotions, mindset, and spiritual life. While aging naturally brings physical changes, how one approaches self-care can significantly affect mental health, confidence, and social engagement.

A. Nurturing Habits for a Healthy, Dignified Appearance

Caring for one's appearance is not about vanity but about maintaining dignity, self-respect, and well-being. Small, consistent efforts can lead to greater confidence and emotional stability.

i. Dressing with Care and Self-Respect

- **Dressing well is a form of self-care**—it affects how one feels and interacts with the world.
- Choosing **clean, well-fitting, and comfortable clothes** helps maintain self-esteem.
- Avoiding **neglect or extreme indifference to dressing** can prevent feelings of stagnation or isolation.
- **Biblical perspective:** Jesus praised **being presentable and honoring the body** (Matthew 6:17—"When you fast, anoint your head and wash your face").

ii. Personal Grooming and Hygiene as an Expression of Self-Value

- **Maintaining essential grooming**—haircuts, skin care, brushing teeth, trimming nails—fosters **a sense of dignity**.
- **Avoiding personal hygiene and care** can indicate deeper emotional struggles, such as depression or withdrawal.
- Regular **self-care rituals enhance mental health**, contributing to feelings of renewal and self-worth.

iii. Posture, Movement, and Facial Expressions

- **Good posture and movement** help maintain a sense of youthfulness and self-assurance.
- A **smile and bright eyes** often reflect a positive mindset, while a perpetual frown or slouched posture can signal discouragement.

- The **mind-body connection** is powerful—acting joyful and upright reinforces emotional resilience.

iv. The Role of Color and Aesthetics in Mood

- Colors and styles can influence mood—wearing bright or warm colors can uplift the spirit, while dull, overly worn-out clothing may subconsciously reinforce a sense of decline.
- Keeping the living environment tidy and aesthetically pleasing (even in small ways) contributes to mental clarity and well-being.

B. Damaging Habits That Reflect Declining Mental Health

Just as positive self-care fosters joy and confidence, certain habits signal emotional or psychological struggles. These should not be ignored, as they often indicate deeper mental and spiritual needs.

i. Neglecting Appearance as a Sign of Emotional Withdrawal

- A **sudden lack of interest in grooming** or dressing properly can be an early indicator of depression or social disengagement.
- Changes such as **staying in nightwear all day, wearing the same clothes repeatedly, or neglecting hygiene** may reflect the loss of motivation or self-worth. Some people give the excuse, "I am not going out, nor is anyone visiting me today. So this is okay." **No, it is not okay.** Whether you go out

or stay home, your appearance should reflect your inner self.

ii. Extreme Obsession with Youthful Appearance

- **Trying to 'defy aging at all costs'**—through excessive cosmetic procedures or an unhealthy fixation on looking young—can be a sign of denial and inner insecurity.
- While **caring for oneself** is healthy, placing self-worth solely on appearance leads to emotional distress.
- Aging gracefully means **accepting change with dignity,** not fighting against time in fear.

iii. Isolating Oneself from Social Engagement

- **Avoiding gatherings due to insecurity about appearance** reinforces loneliness and emotional decline. Make sure you are well dressed when you go out, especially when you go to church.
- **Caring about appearance** should not be about impressing others but about valuing oneself.

C. Theological Perspective: The Body is the Temple of the Holy Spirit

- **1 Corinthians 6:19-20** reminds us that our bodies are

temples of the Holy Spirit, meant to be cared for, not neglected.

- **Aging gracefully does not mean neglecting the body**— it means honoring it appropriately at every stage of life.
- **Jesus Himself took care of His appearance**— Scripture notes that His garments were significant enough that soldiers cast lots for them (John 19:23-24).

D. Practical Encouragement: Finding Balance in Self-Care

- **Small, consistent habits**—a fresh haircut, wearing joyful colors, staying active—make a significant impact.
- **Balance is key**—avoiding both **excessive neglect and excessive vanity.**
- **Confidence and joy are more attractive than youthfulness**—one's inner light and presence truly leave an impression on others.

Conclusion: Age with Grace, Confidence, and Purpose

Appearance is not about vanity—it is about dignity. It reflects **self-respect, mental health, and spiritual dignity**. By caring for oneself while embracing the natural process of aging, one reflects joy, confidence, and gratitude for life.

Chapter 44
Caregiving for the Aged

C aregiving is a crucial aspect of support as people get to the stage of being unable to do everything themselves. It is not uncommon for children to encourage their parents to go live with them at that stage. However, many older adults wish to remain in their own houses as they age. Some people feel uncomfortable sleeping in another place and on another bed. They would insist that they go back to their own home and bed. This is partly because they are familiar with everything in their house, including their regular route from bed to bathroom. In the new place, they are likely to get confused. Therefore, children should understand their concerns and may have to take them back to their house if they insist.

Long-term caregiving requires thoughtful planning and support on the part of family members. It is often undertaken by family members, friends, or professional caregivers. Recognize the importance of supporting them with resources, respite care, and emotional support.

· · ·

Once people are bedridden, home modifications may be necessary to ensure safety and accessibility. Finally, in-home services must be arranged for assistance with daily tasks, medical care, and companionship. Technology such as emergency alert systems, medication reminders, and other communication devices may have to be made available for safety and independence.

Caregiving, whether with trained caregivers or through professional institutions, is not about leaving your loved ones to others. They are still your family members, and nothing can replace the caring love of beloved people. At this point, younger family members have a crucial role to play. Their involvement is not just a duty but a testament to the value and respect they hold for their elders.

Intergenerational connections enrich older people's lives and are a learning moment for the younger generation. Therefore, it shouldn't be considered a burden. If an intergenerational rapport has already been built up, it becomes easier. It's not just at the end of a parent's life that intergenerational get-togethers should happen, but long before it. Educating the young generation about aging is necessary to promote understanding, empathy, and respect for older people. Their active participation in these connections is beneficial not only for the elders but also for their own personal growth and understanding.

Finally

The aging process becomes fulfilling in the context of family, community, and relationships. First, recognize the vital roles of family, friends, and faith communities. Address the practical aspects of caregiving, such as where they are taken care of and how to foster intergenerational connections. Most importantly, stay connected and be proactive in seeking and providing support. Create and embrace the opportunities for meaningful relationships and community engagement to make the golden years sparkling with joy and contentment.

Chapter 45
Ministering to the Elderly

I n the heart of every parish lies a treasure of wisdom, faith, and experience—the senior members of our community. They have weathered the storms of life, embraced the joys and sorrows, and carried the light of faith through the years. Ministering to older people is not just a duty; it is a profound privilege and an opportunity to honor their legacy while enriching our own spiritual journey.

When you consider the lives of the seniors in your parish, you'll realize they possess a wealth of professional expertise, career experience, and deep-rooted faith. Many of them were once highly engaged in parish ministries, dedicating their time, skills, and wisdom to the service of the Church.

In my pastoral ministry, I have been blessed by the invaluable contributions of such remarkable individuals. Their knowledge and expertise have been instrumental in shaping Developmental and Pastoral Renewal Projects that we undertook.

Their professional backgrounds and career experiences proved to be providentially available in areas where I lacked expertise, often becoming the guiding hands that helped turn vision into reality.

Seniors are not merely recipients of ministry—they are an untapped resource, capable of mentoring, advising, and actively contributing to the Church's mission. By recognizing and utilizing their gifts, parishes can create meaningful opportunities for seniors to continue serving purposefully, enriching the faith community in countless ways.

As they enter their golden years, every parish community needs to keep two things in mind. The first, and often immediate, concern for parish leadership is how we can support them at this stage of life. This is a crucial consideration. However, there's another side to the coin. We often fail to recognize the value they bring to the parish community. Their expertise can significantly contribute to the growth of the younger generation and can be a valuable asset to the parish itself. The following ideas are rooted in this twofold awareness.

The Call to Serve

The Church, guided by Christ's teachings, calls us to serve the least among us and to offer compassion, love, and dignity to those in their later years. This ministry for the elderly goes beyond providing physical care; it involves spiritual nourishment, emotional support, and the affirmation of their invaluable contributions to the Church and society.

Building Relationships

Building genuine, heartfelt relationships is at the core of ministering to older people. These relationships are grounded in respect, empathy, and a deep understanding of their unique needs and experiences. Visiting older people, whether in their homes or nursing facilities or bringing them in during parish events, creates opportunities to listen to their stories, share their achievements and joys, and offer solace in times of need.

Practical tips for building these relationships include asking open-ended questions, showing genuine interest in their lives, and being patient and understanding.

Listening with Love: One of our greatest gifts is our time and attentive listening. Each conversation is a sacred encounter, a chance to hear the wisdom and life lessons they have gathered over the years. We affirm their value and dignity through active listening and gain insights to guide our lives.

Celebrating Their Lives: Organizing events that celebrate the lives and milestones of elderly parishioners fosters a sense of belonging and appreciation. Birthday celebrations, anniversaries, and special Masses dedicated to their intentions are beautiful ways to honor their presence in the community.

Spiritual Nourishment

As older people face the challenges of aging, their spiritual needs often become more pronounced. Providing opportunities for spiritual growth and connection is not just essential; it's a responsibility to minister to them. It shows that we care for their holistic well-being and are committed to nurturing their spiritual life.

Regular Sacramental Access: It is vital to ensure that older people have regular access to the sacraments, especially the Eucharist and the Anointing of the Sick. With the help of Eucharistic ministers and organizing transportation for the homebound, Pastoral outreach ensures that they remain connected to the life-giving grace of the sacraments.

Prayer and Devotion: Encouraging personal and communal prayer practices helps nurture their spiritual life. Organizing prayer groups, rosary sessions, and scripture study tailored to their needs creates a supportive environment for spiritual enrichment.

Spiritual Direction and Counseling: Offering spiritual direction and counseling can provide guidance and support as seniors navigate the complexities of aging, illness, and life transitions. These sessions can help them find peace, purpose, and a deeper relationship with God. Parish-based ministry for seniors, or 'Grandparents Ministry,' as they call it in some parishes, is the best platform to offer such opportunities.

Creating a Supportive Community

Ministering to older people requires a collective effort from the entire parish community. Creating a culture of support and inclusion is not just a good idea; it's a necessity. It ensures they feel valued and loved, fostering a sense of belonging.

Intergenerational Programs: Fostering connections between older people and younger generations enriches both groups and strengthens the fabric of our community. Programs that bring together youth and seniors for activities, storytelling, and shared projects create bonds that transcend age and build a stronger, more cohesive community.

For instance, a **'Grandparents Day'** event where seniors share their life experiences with the youth or a 'Youth Mentorship' program where seniors teach practical skills to the younger generation can be excellent examples of such programs. Besides helping with intergenerational bonding, such occasions provide the younger generation with a wealth of practical knowledge and awareness, fostering a sense of community and shared responsibility.

Volunteer Networks: Establishing volunteer networks within the parish can provide practical assistance, such as help with errands, home maintenance, and companionship. Training volunteers to be sensitive to the specific needs of older people ensures that their contributions are compelling and compassionate. Parish organizations such as the Men's Club and Women's Guild, known for their strong community ties and organizational skills, can take the initiative to organize these networks and ensure their smooth operation.

In Summary

Ministering to the elderly in a parish context profoundly expresses Christ's love and compassion. It honors their lifetime of faith, wisdom, and service while enriching the spiritual fabric of the entire community. **By building relationships, providing spiritual nourishment, and creating a supportive environment, we can ensure that the elderly feel cherished, respected, and embraced by the love of Christ.**

Living Well, Aging Well

As we consider embarking on this ministry, let us remember Jesus' words in **Matthew 25:40**: "Truly I tell you, whatever you did for one of the least of these brothers and sisters of mine, you did for me." In serving the elderly, we serve Christ himself, and in their eyes, we glimpse the beauty of a life lived in faith and grace.

Chapter 46
Workshop Ideas for Senior Groups

Here is a variety of engaging activities for seniors that can be used in a parish setting or other community centers that cater to the welfare of people in their twilight years. Some parishes have organizations like the Senior Citizen's Forum or Grandparents Ministry. The following activities promote social interaction, mental stimulation, and spiritual growth among seniors, positively impacting their lives. These activities are not set in stone; they can be adapted and developed to suit each group's particular needs and occasions, allowing group leaders to be flexible and responsive to the changing dynamics of their seniors.

Many group leaders often ponder what to do when they regularly meet. However, by incorporating the following activities into a long-term plan, they will discover a world of endless possibilities for their gatherings, inspiring them to create engaging and diverse experiences for their seniors.

Ice Breakers

1. **Two Truths and a Lie:** Each participant shares two

true statements and one false one about themselves. Others guess which is the lie.

2. **Name That Tune:** Play the first few seconds of a song and have participants guess the title and artist.
3. **Desert Island Choices:** Ask what three items they'd take to a desert island and why. This can lead to interesting and humorous discussions.
4. **Show and Tell:** Bring an item of personal significance and share its story with the group.
5. **Favorite Quotes:** Share a favorite quote or saying and explain why it is meaningful.

Group Dynamic Ideas

1. **Memory-Sharing Circles:** Each participant shares a cherished memory or life lesson. This fosters connection and mutual respect.
2. **Themed Dress-Up Days:** Choose a theme (e.g., 1950s, holiday attire) and encourage everyone to dress accordingly. This can lead to nostalgic discussions and laughter.
3. **Book Club:** Select a book to read and discuss monthly. Include a mix of genres and authors, both contemporary and classic.
4. **Craft Workshops:** Engage in simple, accessible crafts such as card making, painting, or knitting. Provide all necessary materials.
5. **Music and Sing-Along Sessions:** Play favorite tunes from their youth and encourage singing along. This can evoke pleasant memories and create a joyful atmosphere.

Group Discussion Themes

1. **Faith Journeys:** Share personal stories of faith and how it has evolved over the years.
2. **Acts of Kindness:** Discuss small acts of kindness they've experienced or performed and the impact these had.
3. **Historical Events:** Reflect on significant historical events they've lived through and how these shaped their lives.
4. **Health and Wellness:** Share tips and experiences on maintaining physical and mental health in later years.
5. **Hobbies and Passions**: Discuss hobbies they enjoy and how these contribute to their sense of purpose and joy.

Brainteasers and Mental Stimulation

1. **Word Games:** Crosswords, word searches, and anagrams. Provide puzzles that can be done individually or in small groups.
2. **Trivia Quizzes:** Create trivia questions on a variety of topics such as history, literature, and pop culture.
3. **Story Starters:** Give a sentence or two to start a story and let participants continue it, verbally or in writing.
4. **Riddles and Logic Puzzles:** Share fun riddles and logic puzzles that can be solved together, fostering teamwork and critical thinking.
5. **Memory Games:** Play games that test memory, such as matching pairs or recalling details from a short story read aloud.

Special Themes and Activities

1. **Guest Speakers:** Invite speakers on topics of interest such as local history, health, or spiritual growth.

2. **Seasonal Celebrations:** Celebrate holidays and seasons with themed activities, decorations, and foods.
3. **Intergenerational Activities:** Partner with local schools or youth groups for shared activities like storytelling, crafting, or music.
4. **Movie Nights:** Watch classic films together and discuss them afterward.
5. **Cooking Demonstrations:** Invite someone to demonstrate recipes, with opportunities to taste and cooking tips.

Conclusion

As we come to the close of exploring the theology of aging, we pause to reflect on the journey that has brought us to this moment—a journey of discovery, growth, and transformation that has unfolded with grace and gratitude. In the tapestry of life's experiences, we have encountered moments of joy and sorrow, triumph and tribulation, laughter and tears. Yet through it all, we have discovered that aging is not a burden to be borne but a sacred pilgrimage of the soul—a journey that invites us to embrace the fullness of our humanity with courage, wisdom, and grace.

Throughout our journey, we have encountered the rich tapestry of biblical wisdom, the transformative power of community and care, the profound promise of hope and an eschatological perspective. We have explored the depths of our hearts, confronted our fears and uncertainties, and discovered the boundless reservoirs of strength, resilience, and love within us. In the process, we have come to recognize that aging is not a destination but a journey—a journey of continual growth, discovery, and renewal that unfolds with every breath we take and every step we make.

As we bid farewell to these pages, may our hearts be filled with

Conclusion

gratitude for the gift of life, the beauty of aging, and the abiding presence of the divine in every moment. May we carry with us the wisdom of the ages, the compassion of community, and the hope of eternity as we journey forward with courage and grace. May our lives be a testament to the enduring power of faith, hope, and love to transform the world and usher in the Kingdom of God here and now.

With hearts full of gratitude and spirits renewed with hope, let us embrace the journey ahead with open hands and hearts, trusting in the promise of life's eternal embrace and the boundless love that holds us all in its tender care.

THE END IS NOT YET.......

Bibliography

1. Jonathan Westpool - "The Mind-Body Problem - MIT Press Essential Knowledge series

2. Neighbors who care Network- 'Unlocking the Mind'
3. Senex Memory Advisors - Syed Rizvi 'Understanding Cognitive Decline'
4. Fabian - Blog Post - 'Motivation Vs Discipline
5. Fitness Goal 4 U, December 2024
6. "Suffering Depression? So did God's Prophet Elijah" Dr. Mark Riley, co-founder and executive director of SoulCare Counseling.
7. The Serenity Prayer - Reinhold Niebuhr, a Lutheran theologian (1892–1971)
8. Bible quotations - The Catholic Public Domain Version of the Sacred Bible - Ronald L. Conte Jr.
9. Assistance by Grammarly & ChatGPT

About the Author

Rev. Jose Kallukalam was born, educated, and ordained a priest in Kerala, India. He pursued graduate studies in 'Religious Communication' at Loyola University of Chicago before returning to his home diocese, where he served as Director of Communication Media. In this role, he produced television programs and stage productions and penned hundreds of song lyrics, many of which can be found on his YouTube channel, Harmony of Life.

About the Author

His passion for integrating pastoral leadership with communication and administration led him to serve as a Visiting Professor at a major seminary in Kerala, where he taught *Pastoral Communication* —a course blending management principles with pastoral ministry.

With 50 years of priestly ministry, including the years as a pastor in the Diocese of St. Augustine, Florida, Fr. Jose successfully applied strategic planning principles to build thriving, mission-driven parishes. His book, 'Mission-Driven Pastoral Ministry,' is a practical guide and a testimony of how he served at St. Michael's Church, Fernandina Beach.

Also by the Author

A Candle for Father Joe

A deeply moving story of love, loss, and redemption.

A novel drawn from the author's pastotal ministry in which he brings deeply human characters to life.

This is an emotionally powerful novel of a priest who made an impossible choice that transformed a young woman.

The Flame and the Lion

Rome Roared, The Church Whispered Back

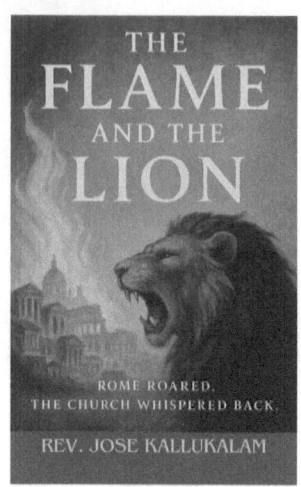

A Historical Novel about

an unknown disciple of Jesus Christ.

Set in the shadow of Roman empire's greatest persecution, this is the untold story of the early Church—not through heroes and miracles, but through memory, faith, and the courage of the voiceless.